"In this account of hellish injury and harrowing recovery, Linnell dramatizes his belief that 'the question—how to live—is a question to ask and not to avoid.' You can never again be exactly who you were an instant ago, but this engrossing book shows how to bear up and live in-between the inescapability of what was and the uncertainty of what is to come." —**Christina Crosby**, author of *A Body, Undone: Living on After Great Pain*

"A revelatory, astounding memoir of overcoming enormous odds, Linnell's tale expertly describes his harrowing recovery following a catastrophic spinal cord injury. With insight and artfully written prose peppered with poetry, he explores the challenges and triumphs of his journey past severe physical affliction. This is an amazing story of resilience and resurrection that is moving, witty, and inspirational." —**Ashok Rajamani**, author of *The Day My Brain Exploded: A True Story*

"His spine may be ravaged but his vision is clear. His prose is simple and impatient, always leaning forward as if eager to get to the next idea, the next image, the next step. He may not be able to walk, but he's always a step or two ahead of the reader, which is the secret of a page-turner . . . If the definition of art is to turn human experience, no matter how distressing, into something beautiful, Jim Linnell has produced not only a work of art but a manual for survival. We are all richer for his achievement." —**Marshall Brickman**

"This profoundly literate memoir of courage stuns and moves, and in its ferocious honesty, delights as few books have over a lifetime of reading the true and fearless sagas of relative strangers who become intimate soulmates." —**Mark Medoff**, Tony award-winning playwright, Oscar-nominated screenwriter of *Children of a Lesser God*

"*Take It Lying Down* by Jim Linnell is a literary tour de force . . . Merciless and merciful, the book speaks to the heart from a place of great wisdom and understanding . . . a profoundly deep and thoughtful and moving book." —**Denise Chávez**, author of *The King and Queen of Comezón*, *A Taco Testimony*, and *Loving Pedro Infante*

"A powerful and gripping life story that inspires, teaches, and transcends the usual autobiography . . . Anyone who is fortunate to know him is blessed, and for those who don't know him please read this book; it's important!" —**Patti Cohenour**, Broadway actress

"Despite great advances in the treatment of spinal cord injuries over the past several decades, there is still no ability to fully restore the functional losses incurred as a consequence of these devastating injuries. At best, we are able to mitigate the progressive damage to the spinal cord, protect the function that remains (if there is any), and afford an opportunity for recovery. Following the first few weeks in the hospital for initial treatment, patients then embark on a long, arduous course of rehabilitation that lasts for months and even years. Unfortunately, a complete recovery never really happens. Jim Linnell's biography beautifully captures the challenges, failures, and victories of that deeply personal and brutal journey. His narrative offers us a first-hand account of the viscerally disturbing (no pun intended) effects of surviving through the aftermath of a spinal cord injury, and the unwelcome but enlightening transformation from one life remembered to a life of unexpected challenges. His work afforded me even greater sensitivity and appreciation for the true people who endure these injuries, for their will to survive, and their new outlook on life." —**Andrew Patterson, M.D.**, Adult Orthopaedic Spine Surgery, University of New Mexico School of Medicine

"A deep and intimate look into one man's journey navigating spinal cord injury. Jim invites you into his story, helping the reader appreciate the resilience of the human spirit and the importance of relationships during challenging circumstances. Jim is an artful storyteller; this book is a poetic reflection of heartbreak, struggle, hard work, and restoration." —**Meghan Joyce, PT, DPT, NCS**, Craig Hospital

Take It Lying Down

FINDING MY FEET AFTER
A SPINAL CORD INJURY

Jim Linnell

Foreword by Len Jenkin

PAUL DRY BOOKS
Philadelphia 2019

First Paul Dry Books Edition, 2019

Paul Dry Books, Inc.
Philadelphia, Pennsylvania
www.pauldrybooks.com

Printed in the United States of America

ISBN 978-1-58988-135-8

Library of Congress Control Number: 2019944415

For Jennifer
And our boys, Hadrian, Jason, and Matt
who took the ride, bumps and all

Contents

Foreword

Len Jenkin

YOU WILL NOT HAVE read another book like Jim Linnell's *Take It Lying Down*. It is a movingly intricate weave—a detailed and poetic chronicle of healing against all odds, an intense love story, a narrative of a young man's journey from Maine to New Mexico and adulthood, and a book of literary inspiration and wisdom, touching on *Electra*, *Heracles*, Mike Leigh's *Topsy-Turvy*, Hieronymus Bosch, and Samuel Beckett, among others.

Late in a successful literary and academic life, Linnell went to Baja California on a family vacation. On the first night in their rented house he stepped off the porch into an unseen hole. The fall left Linnell a quadriplegic with a severe incomplete spinal cord injury. He was told that he might be able to regain some movement—no one could say how much—and the only thing the specialists seemed certain of was that any recovery he might make would happen within two years.

Take It Lying Down describes the struggle of those two years, and documents Jim Linnell's determination to improve. It is also an account of the extraordinary commitment of those around him. These efforts, and a powerful measure of Grace and Mercy, allowed him to walk again, drive a car, take international trips, and continue writing and living in his house off the bosque in Albuquerque's South Valley.

"Poor sap, he forgot there's more to know in that old dumb show, so common is his lot, when least expected comes a twisted plot." A rhyming quatrain concealed in prose introduces the first "Act" of the book, and gives us a hint that this is not a medical book, not a self-help book: it's a literate, occasionally theatrical, surprisingly buoyant, always philosophical and compelling journey through one man's life.

Jim's life-long immersion in the arts, as poet, actor, director of a dramatic writing program, is evident in his prose: bits of plays and poems and wild imagery surface throughout the text, illuminating his experiences and memories. He always keeps his sometimes rapid shifting between forms and his exuberant play with language at the service of truth, and his perhaps unconventional approach to what might otherwise be a straightforward medical memoir leads the reader toward a deep understanding of life's inevitable and sometimes overwhelming sorrows and disasters.

> As we fly out of Albuquerque toward Denver we fly past mountains named Sangre de Cristo. The devil mashed against the blood of Christ. It feels like a Hieronymus Bosch painting. My body feels like a scene with devils dancing around a fiendish device constructed by Christianity's fever dream of sin and its consequences. I am crammed into a drawer made of wire mesh. My nose sticks through a gap on one end and my toes poke out of the other, my body tied naked inside. My skin mimics the feeling of devils hopping about with buckets of hot coals and chunks of ice that they throw on top of

the drawer while one jiggles it so they drop through the
wire gaps.

Though it is a chronicle of recovery, Linnell's book
is not simply the sort of familiar, inspirational tale that
can be of little use to those in pain and facing darkness.
Take It Lying Down is a lesson in the ultimate frailty of
our existence on this green earth. The author lived that
frailty himself, and his writing is an honest account of
facing his own suffering. This is no cheerful greeting
card from the hospital, but a detailed and useful notice
from hell.

Linnell knows that "Suffering is a constant companion, an amoral antagonist that shapes and colors every
aspect of our experience once we are in its grip." And yet,
despite whatever pain he may be in, whatever hopeless-
ness invades his mind, his sense of humor never leaves
him. Soon after Linnell returns home from the hospital, as he and his wife Jennifer are learning to navigate
their new life, the piece of equipment that lifts Linnell's
largely immobile body onto the toilet breaks: "Skipping
the bowel program is not a good idea. If you're squeamish, look away. The only option is old school. On your
side, soldier, do it in the bed. The romance of my injury
never stops. You can look now, I'm dressed."

You will search this book in vain for the kind of self-
pity you might expect, or the kind of anger. What you
will find, again and again, is gratitude—Jim Linnell's
profound gratitude to all those who helped him on his
way, and above all, to Jennifer, for whom his depth of
appreciation and love goes beyond any words even this
wonderfully articulate man can find.

We don't get out of this world alive. If we're lucky, age
will take us on. Unlucky, we are prey to disease, acci-

dent, war, physical and/or mental life-destroying trauma. That's our life. The fiddler will have his money—but that doesn't mean you should stay off the dance floor. Linnell takes us down into the blood and shit, and drags us through it with him. It may not be a joyous ride, but Jim gets us there in the end, his wife Jennifer beside him, the dogs chasing each other through the house, sunshine at the window, sand cranes flying high over the Rio Grande.

The final chapter is an elegiac ode to our life, to the ordinary days and drinks and words and bodies and birds and green growing things. Linnell tells us:

> That one bad thing happens does not change the fact that one good thing happens, that these circumstances occur next to each other by seconds. There is no logic or belief that makes sense of this. There is only persistence, patience, and the wonder of our connection to others who miraculously love us as we love them. Is this enough to keep us in the game, a game we know has no certain rules?

Linnell's answer to his own question is a deeply felt and carefully considered YES.

We hang by a thread, and that thread is so, so beautiful. He doesn't want to be called a hero. Too late for that, Jim.

Accord, New York
January 2019

Take It
Lying Down

Oh well, what does it matter, that is what I always say, so long as one . . . you know . . . what is that wonderful line . . . laughing wild . . . something something laughing wild amid severest woe.

—Samuel Beckett, *Happy Days*

Alas, alas! This is it indeed, all clear.
Here is my sorrow visible, before me.

—Sophocles, *Electra*

Most people think great God will come from the sky
Take away everything, and make everybody feel high
But if you know what life is worth
You would look for yours on earth
And now you see the light
You stand up for your right, yeah

—Bob Marley, *Get Up Stand Up*

Act One

||||||||||||||||||||||||||||||||||||||||||||||||||||||||||||||

In which a kid from Maine, born just before his country enters the Second World War, keeps a clean nose and a dirty mind, executes a coup to seize leadership of a Cub Scout den in the 1950s, comes of age, misses the Drop-Out-Here sign in the whacked-out sixties, sees his country start a war for no lasting purpose and kill people they know nothing about, and is educated at some of the finest schools while remaining ignorant of the basic facts of life. At the threshold of his golden years he's sure he's learned a thing or two from life's hard knocks. Love has turned him inside out. Poor sap, he forgot there's more to know in that old dumb show, so common is his lot, when least expected comes a twisted plot.

CHAPTER ONE
You've Got a Nerve

I LEARN A basic rule of happiness: admit what you don't know when you are naked.

Strapped down, I am easy prey for the winter air. The ground is splotchy with snow and ice where the plane rolls to a stop. The small jet has landed at the Denver airport, four hundred miles north and colder than where I was loaded aboard in Albuquerque. When they pop the door open, cold air rushes inside. It finds me and sends my mangled nerves into spasm. Coming out seems even more precarious than going in because I can see the ground as they twist and tilt the stretcher. All the while they chat about the maneuver and their footing, going slowly. My wife, Jennifer, watches as I am placed in an ambulance waiting to deliver me to Craig Hospital. Once there, I am rolled through automatic doors and taken to the floor for patients with spinal cord injuries. I qualify. I am a quadriplegic from an injury, my breathing assisted by an oxygen tube in my nose, receiving food through another tube threaded up my nose into my stomach, a tracheotomy hole cut in the base of my throat with a plastic insert that renders me speechless. The blood traveling through my veins is flailing on the ropes like a flat-footed boxer, his bob and weave gone.

Jennifer walks next to me. She is unplugged from her life in Albuquerque. She's found sitters for our two Labs and our house so she can come live in a little apartment provided by the hospital for the caregivers and families of patients. My son, Matt, and her son, Jason, are driving her car packed with suitcase, iPad, white-noise machine, and sleeping mask up Interstate 25, over Raton Pass, through Trinidad, Colorado, past Pikes Peak to join us at the hospital.

After I am settled in a room, the first person I encounter on the Craig staff is from the Respiratory Division. She is robust, bristling with efficiency, armed with a computer, and trailed by an assistant in training. She looks like she belongs in a British movie set during the Second World War, the scene where a wounded hero, lost to himself, is taken in hand by a matronly nurse crisp with authority and competence. She shines with her mission—to get me off the breathing apparatus. She is there to determine how long that will take and how much trouble it will be. Because of my injury my intercostal muscles are not in play; my lungs don't fully inflate, so they collect fluid and I start to wheeze and gurgle. She introduces me to a technique to remove fluid from under-inflated lungs, which I am to expect frequently until she declares victory. I experience this technique as a combination of God's finger and septic tank pumping. At the tracheotomy site she pops off the cover of my trachea, which allows her to slip a slender, straw-like probe through the hole into a pool of goo where air should be. This feels like God's digit has slid through my skin and touched a spot so vulnerable and intimate it's a violation, and I convulse in a spasm of coughing. She beams at my strong cough; it will be an ally in my fight to breathe on my own. As I cough up lung slime, the team engages the pumping mechanism to suck out the fluid as it comes within reach of their hose nozzle. Until I can breathe without an assist, this will become a routine. A respiratory nurse will appear like a bad dream, jarring me awake to send me into coughing fits or force an atomized medicine into my lungs. In anticipation of my needs, the first nurse pops a Passy Muir valve in my trachea and I can talk. I want to kiss her.

First was breath. Next is managing my body. I have a nurse and a person called a tech. The nurse monitors my vitals, dispenses my meds, and responds to distress. The tech dresses and undresses me, feeds me breakfast as if I am a baby on solid foods, showers me, and is skilled in managing my bowels. Techs in teams of two or three come to my room during the night to turn my body to different positions like a chicken on a spit. I'm held by a system of pillows and foam squares to prevent bedsores. This is an obsession of my new caretakers, enforced with freeze-your-blood talks and illustrated pamphlets on the consequences of bedsores. Essential to making any of this work with a quadriplegic is a hoist system. A metal track runs around the ceiling above my bed in the shape of a rectangle. A curved metal bar dangles from a wire slotted in the track. To move me, a tech arranges a canvas sling under me that hooks to the curved metal bar. As the bar rises, my body nestles into the fabric of the sling like a measure of dry goods being bagged and weighed. Once lifted in the air I can slide along the track and be lowered into a wheelchair or a shower chair. If I have any delusion that I'm not a quadriplegic, this maneuver dispels any lingering disbelief. The feeling of being meat for measure never leaves me when I'm moved this way.

I SHOULD NOT be here. I should be opening the college meeting that starts the semester. To know why I
am here—out of all the possible fates for a man planning his retirement—will take several steps to explain.
I'll start with what happened after the surgery for my
neck injury, which will mean rewinding the clock back
a week. A week ago was early January of the new year,
2012. I'd been in the ICU at the University of New Mexico Hospital recovering for almost twelve days. A woman
dressed in 1950s chic like a new teacher at the Hogwarts
Academy comes to visit me. She's bright and cheery and
full of questions for Jennifer and me, as if I am applying
to be her new student. It is my good luck that my surgeon spent time early in his career at Craig Hospital, one
of the leading rehab centers for spinal cord injury in the
country. He says that is the best place for me to go after
my surgery. The cheery woman quizzing me has flown
here from Denver to decide if I am a good bet for Craig
to invest time in rehabbing me and teaching me to manage my injury. When she looks at me she sees a seventy-
year-old man who is a quadriplegic from an injury to his
spinal cord. The injury is labeled incomplete because the
piece of bone that touched my spinal cord only made a
small dent. In the spinal-cord-injury lottery my ticket
says Good for a Chance for Uncertain Amount of Return
of Bodily Function.

Any touch on the spinal cord is like Spock's Vulcan
nerve pinch. As the spinal cord goes into shock, immedi-
ate paralysis results. A penetration deeper into the cord,
along with the formation of scar tissue, usually closes off
any nerve traffic past that point, and the injury is called
complete, with no chance for return of function. The
woman from Craig exudes confidence, in that post-war
sense, that the Americans have landed. She is looking at

me but also at Jennifer as my primary caregiver, to see if we are ready to face our fight and play the roulette of spinal cord return, a game with no clear outcome and certainly more heartbreak than victory. Jennifer is fit, a former dancer with a muscular will, a sixth sense about her body, and a lifelong discipline of training and overcoming pain. We should come to Denver. Oh, and plan for a stay of at least three months.

I can't say "I'm a quadriplegic" and know what that means. My stay in the ICU felt surreal. I wouldn't have been surprised if a giraffe came into my room and sang sea chanteys about flying fish and Shangri-la. I had some small movement in my right hand, but my body felt like a foreign object; its only other movements were involuntary spasms in my legs. I could only focus on being hurt, that I'd had an operation, and that there was a place to go where I might get better. Being paralyzed was a fact I couldn't deny but didn't let my mind admit. I easily held these two contrary realities next to each other as I was packed up to travel to Denver on a medevac flight. It was my second medevac flight in two weeks. I live in Albuquerque, so the first flight began somewhere else on the map.

The "somewhere else" came about when the phone rang one early evening in September. It was my son Matt. I answer in the house where Matt, as a four-year-old, hitched along the brick floors in his cowboy boots, six-shooters, and red cowboy hat. Jennifer and I are sitting on a small porch by the kitchen letting the view of the Manzano Mountains slowly still the buzz of the day. We are discussing what we'll do in six months when I retire from the university where I'll have worked for thirty-seven years. Jennifer will have beaten me across the finish line by a year when I break the tape. Waiting,

I'm like a cocktail placed on a windowsill to be tasted at leisure when that time comes. The windowsill in this house isn't the narrow wooden kind I grew up with in Maine, but a wide stucco ledge that is part of an opening punched in a wall made of mud, in a place settled before the Pilgrims knew there was a Plymouth Rock. The light wind that comes through the window travels over a two-acre landscape that bundles together a big lawn, a field, raised vegetable beds, a courtyard and fountain, a small fish pond, old cottonwoods, a sycamore the size of Vesuvius, a small orchard, and flower gardens throughout. This feat of gardening has been our sustained obsessive pleasure as a couple since we were married. When we started, it was a blank canvas, mostly weeds and dirt, and we never tire of filling in and revising.

Matt calls, excited to enlist us in a plan to celebrate his fortieth birthday. He wants the whole family to gather at a small beach town on the Mexican Baja called Todos Santos during the Christmas holidays. In December we will be in gardening withdrawal, with all of nature around us sleeping in shades of brown. The beach and the heat in Baja will be an electric shock to our cold, parched bodies.

We'll go to Mexico to celebrate with Matt, come back, and time will fly until the gold-watch party—and we'll be free. We spin tales to each other about our life in retirement. They include travel requiring a passport, hiking among the wonders of the West, binging on cultural tourism, holing up with writing projects, indulging grandchildren, messing with the inside of our house instead of the outside for a change, indulging each other, slowly tasting the flavors in the cocktail we'd become separately and together. Six months more before I could drink up. The years given over to the university leave no regrets, only pocketed memories: tag you're it, take it from here. I'll step away and the river will plunge on without me.

I was a little uneasy reaching seventy. My father, a wily Yankee trial lawyer who grew up on a farm, died at that age. My lawyer brother, a sentimental hard-ass the size of a linebacker, added three years to my father's total, and my mother, a doctor's only child who majored in French and wrote poetry, never made it past fifty-nine by her own choosing. All in Maine, with fresh-mown hay, lightning bugs, pine forests, lakes, and cribbage. If I forge through the decade and past it, I will be blazing new territory for my family. Jennifer will have no talk of doubt about my blazing. She says this will be our time together, dismissing my caution. She says this while taming some unruly mess in her kitchen. Thinking of my family's history, I say something about genes and how they may get a vote. All 102 pounds of her trim body tense, and her voice, capable of reaching a hundred beginning dancers in a huge gymnasium, pins me where I stand, rejecting my fatalistic talk. She closes her ears to the rule of genes and grips fiercely to healthful eating, exercise, and the power of the mind and body. The house can run for a day on the electricity she summons in beating back my uncertainty.

I have been the dean of the College of Fine Arts for five years at the university that runs the ICU. When I began, I feared the dean job would smother every chance for my own creative work. My response to that panic was to carry a notebook. Whether sitting at lunch, or shopping with Jennifer, or riding in the car, I worked on a series of poems. The pressure was useful, a kind of tonic. Despite all our excited talks about when we will both be free of work demands, we are entering unknown terri-

tory. The trip to Todos Santos will be an appetizer to
what is to come.

In December; suitcases lie flagrantly open in our bedroom. Two black Labs are plastered against the floor,
watching anxiously as we pack. I move around the house
gathering what I want for the trip. The windowsill waits;
I'm ready to mix that cocktail, ready to experiment with
its flavors. I can see light glinting off the glass resting in
the open window.

We fly to LA and on to Cabo San Lucas, where we
connect with Matt, his wife, Amy, and his little girl, Isabel—a picture-perfect young American family. We are
through customs at the airport; the air, thick and warm,
loosens our bones. Car rented, we head for various mar-
kets to provision our stay. Matt and Amy have done this
before and find their way through unfamiliar traffic, for-
age through store aisles, rolling up to the cashier in a
small caravan of carts loaded with staples and liquor. Jennifer's sons' families will arrive later. Cabo is a sprawling
city, a place where cruise ships anchor, releasing tourists
to fill the restaurants and stores around the port, ready
buyers who spread American dollars. We will hole up at
a beach condominium near Todos Santos for three days,
awaiting access to our rental house. The road between
Cabo and our destination is under construction, torn up,
leaving dirt surfaces and random unfinished overpass
constructions that look like a giant's scattered toy set.

The day before we move to the rental house in Todos
Santos, I sit beside a pool at the condo, editing a book
of poems finished in my walkabout time when I wore
my cape and mask as the dean. The impetus to write
the poems is like when a dog seizes a small animal and
shakes until there is nothing left in it. The book roughly
traces a narrative from knowing little about love, to see-

ing it wreck those close to me, to knowing something, then opening to risk and finding there is love that won't break. The poems speak about the itch for happiness and what it means to me to be imprinted by our American landscape.

We drive to the rental house in Todos Santos in two cars, winding through dirt lanes with palm trees, a mixture of garden and desert with high walls surrounding houses with cool, shaded courtyards that evoke enchantment and secrets. Our party has grown to include Jason, his wife, Cindy, and their boys, Tucker and Haarlem; and Hadrian, the oldest of the three step-brothers. He is without his family, who are off skiing in the mountains of Colorado. As we come closer to the beach, vegetation thins and the air blooms with the smell of ocean. We pull into the wide driveway of a compound: large rental house, small rental house, garage, and about fifty yards away, the owner's house. The woman who gave us the deal over the Internet shows us the quirks of the house. We scatter to our different rooms and get settled. It is too early to start cooking dinner. We set off for a walk on the beach to look for whales and soak up the ocean. It is deadly to go swimming along this beach because of the treacherous currents. Our walk has a built-in governor: Isabel, our kinetic, blonde, two-and-a-half-year-old grandchild, is swung along between her parents' hands with cries of "More!" She's in her phase of now joy, now meltdown, her moods washing over her parents like sudden weather. A whale spotted on the horizon lends ancient magic to our new house by the sea.

WHILE MY LUNGS are being assessed, Jennifer unpacks in her nearby apartment with Matt and Jason's help. Soon her boys will go back to their lives. She is a vital woman who holds sway over a large adobe house, the queen of two black Labs, a professor emerita of dance, a master cook and gardener constantly in motion: walking, washing, weeding, watering, cooking, creating, exercising, shopping, and teaching. Now she is stuck in a tiny apartment. Her world has become one of stricken individuals, shadowed by caretakers-to-be like herself; in this new world her husband cannot take her hand or pull her close in an embrace. That husband would have carried the suitcases to her room while she unpacked. Now that husband lies immobile in a hospital room fifty yards away.

I think about what connects us across this distance. I trace a line in my mind from where I grew up, house in the country, horses, pasture, woods, one-room schoolhouse. Then to Lewiston, Maine, across the Androscoggin River to Bates College—colonial brick, history of ideas, an electric girl who touches desire and uncovers poetry, bachelor's English and Philosophy. To New York City. Graduate study in philosophy incomplete—grim classes, seductive city, loneliness. On to Columbus, Ohio, a new plan: a masters program in theater at a school as big as a city, locusts crunch under car tires. Oh so brainy, cooks up a thesis, stages Kafka's *The Trial*, still dumb as a post about emotional anatomy. Makes it over the Rockies, crosses desert to Berkeley. Calendar reads 1965, starts a Ph.D. in directing at a university in upheaval, a helicopter teargasses schoolkids, soldiers with fixed bayonets line the campus entrance. Who's happy? The one who sent the soldiers, Ronnie Reagan. Dates girl in neighboring apartment, families gather in sleepy oil patch town Taft, California, for wedding. Crosses the Atlantic for study in Greece, mother goes missing. Takes handshake for making it to ABD, all but the dissertation. Lightning strikes the jobless. Return to the Midwest, to Northwestern in Evanston, Illinois. A teaching greenhorn, what to make of this? Sperm-in-baby-out experiment works. Baby flying on feet grinning in the air. Trade fat paper on commie symp, Bertolt Brecht, to be a doctor of "nobody will ask you to set their broken leg." Finds exit door and goes south to Indian country. New job, students hungry, first house, finds stride, father goes missing. Night, he and she in a car, a kiss. He and she naked in a sauna. Everything is in reach and nothing is. Which is the right choice, hide or be seen? Seen. Couples stuck together are unstuck. Rice tossed, time speeds. Are our choices found lying about like supplies dropped by travelers gone ahead? Is the path we think new and bravely chosen actually rutted and worn beneath a carpet of windblown debris? What does it matter if we've never known the place where we find ourselves? She unpacks, not naked, in a hospital apartment not far from him, the kinetic body in the sauna unreachable.

We learn the difference between stuck and unstuck is ungoverned change that is blind to the line between thrill and cruel. It is a package that arrives wrapped in plain paper, the address smudged, edges dented by teeth marks. What spills out once seen can't be unseen. Nothing after can stay the same. Our wedding party is next to a sprawling dairy farm. Cows watch, flies pester the guests, a raggedy hound dog joins in, friends are startled seeing a high wire act without a net. Matt, Jason, and Hadrian are six, eight, and ten years old when the couple first step on the wire, five years before the tie-the-knot party lit by a June sun testing its heat.

THE BEACH WALK OVER, the boys prepare supper. They kick Jennifer to the curb as they flex their considerable cooking muscles. It is dark by the time we all sit down to eat. Disney's *Tangled* somehow comes up. The adults break into a dispute over the plot of the Grimm version and how it compares to the Hollywood movie. No Google, so we eventually exhaust our collective ignorance, not getting much beyond the tower, the hair, and the handsome prince. We forget the part about how Rapunzel reveals her secret, how a prince climbs her hair to be with her in all senses of "to be." We forget that the witch casts her out into the wilderness, and how the prince learns he'll never see her again, leaps from the tower and is blinded by thorns below. We don't remember that Rapunzel has twins. They've been busy in the tower. It wouldn't be Grimm without a little grisly mayhem. By then we have emptied our plates and the energy shifts to what's next. Jennifer and I claim elder privilege to escape washing dishes. We announce our intent to go for a walk to see the beach at night. I remember the porch is a jumble of furniture, a table for eating and some chairs. As we open the door to go out, the night is pitch black: no lights in the neighborhood or on the porch or the grounds. We are momentarily blinded by the dark and feel our way forward, trusting that the steps are straight in front of us. We step onto air and fall three feet to hard ground.

"Dad! Breathe!"

Matt calls as if to someone lost. There is a rush to the owner's house to ask where to find an ambulance. Amy and Cindy are sent to town on the slim hope that one was seen earlier, but warned that none are stationed there. I startle awake, breathe, realize I can't move, and say, "I'm fucked!" Some enchantress, conjured as a harrowing spirit bringing unbound change, seized me in the dark and threw me like Rapunzel's prince down from a stone tower, leaving me immobile.

The wives find luck in the form of an available ambulance, and lead it to the house. I'm strapped to a board, loaded on to go where? The nearest medical facility is in Cabo, sixty miles south. The road between Cabo and Todos Santos is a sprawling, unfinished, bumpy, uneven jumble. They take down our names, Jim and Jennifer; coming with us are Hadrian and Matt. What do I think about during the slow ride that takes nearly an hour? It was more like not thinking. The thought of being paralyzed sat on my brain like a gargoyle beating a drum to stop me from facing what it actually meant. When I can stop the drumbeat I crack open a door to a movie running in a loop, showing scenes from my life. See, all will be as it was. Then a voice cuts in to say, "You didn't just stub your toe, you're really fucked here, hope all you want."

At the medical clinic they take an MRI. Surprisingly, it is not one of those cave-like machines that sounds like it's grinding granite. Instead it looks like a giant mushroom. They position my torso and neck on it. The news from the MRI is trouble. My neck is injured; I must see a surgeon. I need to get to a hospital, but Albuquerque is over 1,100 miles from Cabo. How to get there becomes a maze of obstacles that we have to clear. It takes all night: arrange for a medevac flight and then pay for the ambulance, the treatment at the medical facility, and the medevac flight. That will be 40,000 American dollars please. No pay, no go. Jennifer and the boys play casino with their credit cards. Still no one can leave. The plane won't take off unless a doctor in Albuquerque agrees to admit me to a hospital. Unexpectedly, this becomes difficult. The doctors we know can't do it. The boys begin dialing like crazed slot-machine players until Hadrian calls his father, a sports fanatic and no stranger to injury. He knows a surgeon. The payout bells ring. A doctor found, we are cleared to go.

I am restrapped to the board and stuffed into a plane along with two attendants, Jennifer, and Hadrian. Matt and Jason will follow later. The noise of the engines fills the space like a thick paste. I feel a stinging pain. The back of my head feels like it's resting on a sharp pebble. I ask for help. No one hears. The attendants are near but are talking and pay no attention to my bleats. The plane is small, the vinyl walls and roof are close. My head is throbbing. I'm finally noticed by one of the attendants. He gives me relief with some thin padding. It all feels like I've been tossed in a drawer in a metal fabrication shop. I hear big equipment scrape and vibrate outside my tight cocoon. When we land in Albuquerque the noise stops, the drawer opens. There is no standard way of taking me off the plane. It depends on the size and weight of the patient and the method of the attendants. They carry me to the doorway, then lift my stretcher head up, feet down, one walking backward down the stairs. I see space and ground and nothing in between and grit my teeth. Stowed in a waiting ambulance, we head to the hospital. Just how deep is the trouble I'm in? The answer is in a snapshot, taken at the clinic near the sea while boats bobbed in the moonlight and lovers sighed under the palm trees.

I wake up in an ICU room with a breathing tube, a catheter, and an IV line stuck in my arm. Dr. Paterson is a cross between a rock star and an athlete, with thick, black hair combed straight back, virtuoso hands, and an engaging directness. He quickly decided to operate to prevent further swelling that threatened more damage to my spinal cord. He stabilized my neck at C4-C5 with plates, screws, and rods. The bones fractured on impact when I fell into a depression where a shrub was removed.

Jennifer fell on flat ground. My fractured bones are rein-
forced and reshaped as if I'm a smashed car in a body
shop. I have a neck brace. I'm still in a fog; the facts don't
help. The sense of being stuffed in a drawer that started
in the plane reemerges. Every kitchen has one, that junk
drawer where you toss things no longer useful, not yet
ready to be thrown away.

A wind blossoms in the trees along the river and
rushes through an open window, a cocktail glass on the
wide windowsill tips and falls to shatter on a brick floor.

The drug brew I'm on for pain, inflammation, and
infection sets me loose from the drawer and takes me
deep into a dark wood. My mind dreams, steps off a
ledge, and slips down time like a rope until catching on
a knot. I hear a rooster crow. Everybody is asleep. I slip
on my jeans and a warm top and jam my feet into hiking boots. I slip out the door to the gravel front yard of
a small adobe house, perched in a cut in a hill, beat up
by the weather, by the very sun I step into. A dirt road
wends its way up the hill. The sky jumps out of the horizon and sings blue, a full hallelujah, the air as bracing
as Listerine. Next door is a smaller house with a cement
skin and a curl of smoke coming out the chimney. A
man emerges; he's been warming tortillas on his fire and
waves, offering me one.

Two cars are parked in the yard, our friends' Volks-
wagen camper and my red Volvo. It's the 1965 Volvo, so
not the humpback model, but the boxy version. Sleeping inside the house are two friends, painters who'd
come to Santa Fe from the Bay Area where they'd met
my wife, also sleeping, also a painter. Up the hill a dog
barks. The neighbor's tortillas warm over a piñon wood
fire. Its smoke invades the senses and says, "Where are
you going? What have you got to worry about? Sit. Look

around you." I can smell the dirt in the air. I think, "This is a place to be," nothing in the way of what that verb can mean. Then I think, "Why don't I live here?"

We drove here from Berkeley, on our way to Evanston, Illinois, where I had been teaching at Northwestern. I met my wife Susan, who is still sleeping, in Berkeley during a PhD program in theater directing. When I met her she was disguised as a social worker despite an art degree from Berkeley. I am returning to my second year of teaching. I'd gone back to California for the summer to work on my dissertation, the last thing to finish before getting the three little letters. I'd landed in Berkeley in 1965. I was there for the whole Dionysian pageant: America's children who fled their suburban homes looking for a new enlightenment of feeling collected in drifts on Telegraph Avenue. Students once on track for a degree quit to pursue the new consciousness and tear up all the old rules. The war protests became a fevered contagion of uncivil confrontation; the cultural undressing and its new freedoms were the real drug that scared the elders. The sleeping wife is four months pregnant. The baby floating inside her was conceived by sixties radicalized parents in Deerfield, a suburb of Chicago, seemingly untouched by the change raging across the country.

The next summer, once again heading from California to Evanston for another year of teaching, we arrive in New Mexico like homing pigeons. I am still under the spell of the desert landscape. This time I am driving a large, steel-blue Chevrolet Suburban, a concession to parenthood so we can carry the baby, Matt, back and forth across the country. This time I am on a mission. My work at Berkeley is done. I visit the university in Albuquerque. Do they have a job opening? No. I'd be interested when they do. Nice to know, they say. I am longing for a different geography: one of a wide horizon, light as sharp as broken glass, ceremonial space, dirt houses, and room for art that isn't over-determined by a past.

A letter comes from the university in New Mexico describing a means of escape. Come visit, if we like you we'll send a contract you can use to move from there to here. I get my means of transit to New Mexico. Matt is four. For all those trips back and forth from the West Coast we fitted the blue Suburban with a homemade traveling storage box in place of the back seat. The top had three lids for the storage compartments, and supported a small mattress and crib for Matt when he was a baby. Why does this matter? It was clever and it was evidence of unresolved stress in our relationship. Every measurement, joint, fitting, nail, and screw that went into the making of this box held the tension from our arguments over each step. Its clean functionality presented a deceptive picture of its married makers. If they were terra-cotta figures their surfaces would be fissured with fine cracks. It is 1975 when we find and settle into a rambling, fix-me-up adobe house beside the Rio Grande.

I come west to be in a place where everything isn't already decided. I don't realize that intention will boomerang directly into my personal life. Sitting across the table from me at my first faculty meeting is a blazing energy source. She is dressed in black dance tights with a chrome-yellow sweater draped over her shoulders against the air-conditioning; a deep-red scarf cinched round her head frames her face, a dark brown ponytail bursts out behind. Jennifer is her name. She is the head of the dance program.

Jennifer was trundled to Albuquerque as a little girl by an artist father and a furiously unhappy mother. While her father started the art education department at the university, she grew up a nomad, sent to train in dance studios out of state. Her talent and a cold, determined mother fixed a path that took her to Juilliard and to a ballet career at the Metropolitan Opera. Then the sixties had their way with her. She came to San Francisco when I was in Berkeley, though we never met. She became a modern dancer, performing with Anna Halprin. She married an architect whose career was starting its rocket ride up. His work brought them to Albuquerque and they had two boys, Hadrian and Jason. What they made in San Francisco was not unlike the travel box in the blue Suburban, also built with a craft that could not sustain the tension of its devising.

The ICU dreamer has slid along his rope and dangles from a knot in time tied thirty-two years ago when the two couples break into pieces. The adobe house by the Rio Grande holds two members of the four-person marital wreck. After the daily soap episodes of our falling in love in front of our students and colleagues, a full-on opéra bouffe, our experiment in starting new lives ends with a ring hidden in a sock under a pillow. We raise three boys from cats fighting in a bag to brothers sharing holidays with their families.

I'M AWAKE. The three no-longer boys watch a medical posse surround my bed. They're ready to remove the breathing tube inserted during surgery. I still have a tracheotomy that renders me speechless, as no air can activate my voice box. A respirator assists my breathing. I discover my legs can move, not because I will them to, but because they spasm. Jennifer is in a lost state, different from mine, unmoored. Jason and Matt have joined Hadrian, and they surround her with care, alternate playing watchdog with visitors and nurses, and manage the terrain of fear as best they can. I don't look good. I am fighting a fever from the insult of the surgery and the accident and loss of any sense of agency. The machinery of the hospital thrums like a tropical storm, always threatening to reach hurricane strength. The rain and the wind sweep through my mind, not letting me hold a coherent thought about this evolving disaster movie. My world shrinks to the size of my bed and the storm around it. I feel helpless and afraid.

My accident happened between Christmas and New Year's. It is New Year's Eve. I'm alone in my room. My pharmacological fog persists, smudging my surroundings. Orderlies appear to load me on a gurney and roll me away for some test the doctor ordered. I feel as if I'm in a black and white movie, a kind of noir mystery filmed in dark corridors and basements. I'm sure they stash me in a corner in what feels like a cement alcove. I hear what sounds like a card game and drinking. Behind me, where I can't see, voices joke, celebrate. Time congeals.

I get better. Friends visit, try to read my lips, try to hide their shock at what I look like and what has happened. A month before, I was in a competition for the position of provost. This made me a very public figure, dashing around campus as a player in the eternal drama of faculty politics. I didn't get the job. But it multiplies the number of visitors who come to see me, unbelieving at my sudden change of fortune. The visits are both welcome and unwelcome. Welcome for the outpouring of concern and the pleasure of seeing people who know and love me. Unwelcome in the ways the visits remind me of what is lost, the person who strode around campus in ambitious motion, tilting at grand windmills. Instead, I am flat on my back in a hospital johnny, stuck with tubes beside blinking monitors and watched by an anxious family, silently moving my lips, vainly hoping people can decipher some sense. I am a beached wreck washed up from some distant storm.

I am out of play and Jennifer has lost her grip on what to do or think, upended. Our boys take over the management of our lives. They divide up our world between our funds, insurance, and a lawsuit against the owners of the rental house where I fell. It is a little like getting undressed in front of your grown children as they peer into all your business: your passwords for the computer, everything about your financial situation. But it is also a thrill to watch them become a team, taking care of us with such competence. They jump to the task without skipping a beat. Combined, they are a formidable presence, as if a wing-tipped law firm just swept into the room. I can almost hear the click of their briefcases opening and closing as they deal with problems, talk with university administrators about my future, and toss about the elements of our lives like the ingredients in a recipe that we can dine off until things are better—whenever that will be.

When we flew out of Cabo we flew past a land formation called El Cajón del Diablo, or the devil's drawer. As we fly out of Albuquerque toward Denver we fly past mountains named Sangre de Cristo. The devil mashed against the blood of Christ. It feels like a Hieronymus Bosch painting. My body feels like a scene with devils dancing around a fiendish device constructed by Christianity's fever dream of sin and its consequences. I am crammed into a drawer made of wire mesh. My nose sticks through a gap on one end and my toes poke out of the other, my body tied naked inside. My skin mimics the feeling of devils hopping about with buckets of hot coals and chunks of ice that they throw on top of the drawer while one jiggles it so they drop through the wire gaps. An old crone dances a spastic jig, carrying a sharp stick she erratically jabs into my left shoulder.

When we learn I'll be at Craig for three months I realize Jennifer, too, is being tossed in a drawer. This woman of constant motion will have her life seized as if a solemn devil has her in his grasp. Her body arches, legs flail as she is pushed down while another fiend pours tar into the open drawer sticking her to the bottom. Suddenly pulled from her world and our life together, she is bound to my journey. You would have to be superhuman not to think of it as a kind of hell, despite every effort to hope, to deny as she faces the loss of my animate vitality. I am familiar. It is my six-foot-one body, the face she's kissed, the arms and hands that held and touched her. It's the dreamy guy who worked as fanatically in the yard as she, and who procrastinated until she had a fit. Looking straight at me emptying a grocery bag she'd say, "I do everything you ask me quick quick, just like that, and what about you? Not so quick quick, huh!" There he is and is not. Is he lost or dead? Yet he is right there needing her. It makes grieving complicated.

One of the first issues people with my injury struggle with is some version of "Why me? What did I do to deserve this?" It is a fool's errand, trying to find yourself in a ravaged landscape, pursued for some transgression: greed or pride or sloth. I was guilty of all those things, yet for me this way of thinking holds no force. I was raised in a small New England town. Christianity as practiced by the Congregational Church was gently poured over my head. It shored up my conscience, exposing me to a conflicted mixture of forgiveness and transgression, elevated by the language of my King James Bible that made more of the world than it seemed to be. Then I went to

college, where I discovered the Greeks, their vase paint-
ings, their embrace of the naked body frontal and erect,
and the ferocity of tragedy that never heard of the Garden of Eden. Here was a concept of disaster that was
not a consequence of bad action or the weakness of the
flesh: instead, it is the working of the world that makes
suffering visible and part of the very fabric of humanity. Sophocles's *Oedipus* is evidence of this Greek turn of
mind, as when the chorus looks at the blind Oedipus and
says, "Count no man happy until he is dead." I am also a
Walt Whitman American with an excited confidence of
spirit and self, alive in a landscape of providence. How
does who I am matter now? Can I look at suffering as a
dimension of life, not as punishment? Immobile, can I
still see and hear the world and be in love with it?

We are in completely unknown territory, far from any
meaning of home, deposited in a hospital at the foot of
the Rocky Mountains, unsure if my injury will undo us,
turning the pleasure of living into the maintenance of
existence. Clinging to the new environment as a fantasist
does to the lottery, we push thoughts of tragedy from our
minds. Since the unfinished walk to the beach we have
not spoken alone about what happened. The boys surround Jennifer, and doctors, nurses, and therapists surround me. This conversation has to come.

I ARRIVE AT Craig Hospital in the morning. I could
never have anticipated what happens that afternoon. Jennifer is moving into her apartment and I am lying in
bed trying to take in my new surroundings. Two young
women enter my room. One is blonde and striking and
could have stepped off a Scandinavian Airlines flight.
The other is attractive, with brown hair and an imp hidden in some pocket. They both look as if they're part of a

health cult, just freshened up from a mountain hike. The sight of them, before they say a word, lifts my spirits. They convey a feeling that everything is going to be better. Whatever they think, looking at a seventy-year-old man suddenly made a quadriplegic, never crosses their faces. I could have been twenty and they would've looked at me with the same expectation of "Let's go to work." Caitlin, the blonde, has an easy laugh that takes you out of your shell. She is my occupational therapist. Meghan has the look of, "You and me, buddy, we're going to cook up some crazy shit." She is my physical therapist. They will divide my body between them: everything above the waist belongs to Caitlin, and everything below is the property of Meghan. These two didn't just come to the room to blast their wattage at whatever sad schlub they find staring at the ceiling. Look, we bear gifts. I see a power wheelchair with them and they intend to put me in it to see if I can work the controls.

The lift system in the room is used to expertly bundle me into the sling, hoist me from the bed, and set me in the chair. It is like someone takes a frame showing frozen, greasy, yellowing snow and dead stick-trees and tilts it to reveal blue sky, warm houses, smoke huffing from fat chimneys, and birds animating bare tree limbs. It is liberating, odd as that sounds, to be in a wheelchair. I can operate the controls: to move at all is the best drug. They fuss over adjusting the chair for my posture, then buckle my seat belt so I won't flop onto the floor. They watch long enough to see I'm not a lunatic who will race his chair to bash his head against a wall. Satisfied, they flash their high beams at me and leave me to test my driving skills.

It is a shock. What a difference it makes to sit up and have the agency of movement, even if it is with a machine. Our language is full of expressions of judgment aimed at sloth. Those of weak character are called lay-abouts. Insults fly to kick them to stand up or to convict them of impotence, weakness, laziness, or moral absence. Now I can be with people and not be an object laid out like a fish on a platter. Jennifer and the boys are happy and amazed to see things change so quickly. "Show us," they say. "Come on, Andretti, light up the horses, what have you got?"

I've passed over a detail of the welcome wagon I received when I arrived: the talk where they explain how they will manage my bowels. This is like the space shuttle. How do they take care of that business? Craig has a bowel program to regulate when I go. I choose what time of day I want—morning or evening. They put me in a rolling chair with an open-bottom seat and use an ointment to numb the portal entrance. Then a tech wearing gloves sticks a suppository up my butt. A capture vessel goes under the bottom of the chair. Nature has its way, but that isn't all. I learn a new word I could do without. That word is *dilling*, short for digital rectal stimulation. They stick a gloved index finger up to the first knuckle and rotate around to encourage any remaining treasure to move down the chute. After three insertions of a digit without further action, I'm declared finished. It is remarkably matter-of-fact. I will get used to it as the way things are done. It is essential for all parties to know I can go through my day without fear of an accident. I wasn't always so lucky early on. Part of my learning curve is losing all modesty or shame about my body around strangers.

Jason leaves, bungeed home by his work. Matt will stay until the end of the week to hear the review by my team of doctor and therapists. The work with Caitlin and Meghan starts when they brush me with a feather and stick me with a pin. It isn't some schizo method—see, we like you, no we don't—to break down a patient's resistance, but the American Spinal Injury Association (ASIA) test. The ASIA Impairment Scale is used to define and describe the extent and severity of a patient's spinal cord injury and create one of the benchmarks against which future rehabilitation and recovery will be measured. My grade is based on how much sensation I can feel at multiple points on my body. The test results in a grade from A (most fully impaired) to E (normal). It takes time to go through all the points on both sides of the body using a pin and a feather to record the sensations or lack. Telling me not to look, they touch a point and ask if the feeling is sharp or dull. The women joke that patients often cheat by looking, as if this were a test in school. They might've been reading my mind. They grade me a C, which means some sensation has been spared below the level of injury, but half the muscles below that point cannot move against gravity. Even though I can feel some sensation it doesn't mean I am able to move . . . yet. The *yet* is like a cartoon balloon of positivity above these young women's heads. I will learn they expect me to fill the balloon above my own head with the same positive word.

Before the end of the week I'm scheduled for a separate hour each day in the therapy room with Caitlin and Meghan. They are just getting started finding out what happens when they manipulate my body. They discover the trouble in my left shoulder. It is horribly painful and they call it a frozen shoulder. It calls for a lovely woman to see me twice a week. She uses manipulation and dry needling, an exquisite pain worthy of the skills of Torquemada, to work to unfreeze it. The Hieronymus Bosch scene of the crone stabbing my shoulder with a sharp stick wasn't just a pharma daydream.

Jennifer, Matt, and I find the conference room for my review. The doctor overseeing my case is Dr. Skelza, a man in his forties paralyzed from the waist down by a teenage auto accident, who races around the hospital corridors in his manual wheelchair. It is a pleasure when he rolls up to wherever he finds me each morning. He conveys uplift and confidence that his bag of tricks is bigger than my bag of woes. His first question was about pain. A medicine I don't need is for pain control. By some blessed luck I do not have nerve pain. Instead I say, Please God, stop my St. Vitus dance. Dr. Skelza starts me on the drug baclofen for what becomes an obdurate subplot of my injury story: spasms. The brain sends garbled messages to the muscles, causing strong and sometimes violent contractions. A message starts off all perky, speeding along the spinal cord like a new car, then runs into a jagged pothole at the injury point that wrecks the suspension and the steering. When it reaches its destination, the message is scrambled and the transmission gets stuck in drive, jerking a muscle in a manic repeat. A spasm feels like being screwed by an alien stalker who humps your body without your permission; you stiffen and contract but not with pleasure. The result is fatigue, pain, and lack of sleep, and if the spasms aren't stopped—if I can't throttle the psycho—I'm useless for therapy. Baclofen is used to manage the body's reactions to the garbled messages, but a common side effect is drowsiness. When Meghan lays me on my back on a therapy mat table, she has to monitor my eyes. If they slowly glaze and start to close, she says my name like a knock on my forehead to keep me awake.

The rest of the team around the table includes Meghan and Caitlin, the nurse attached to my room, plus a counselor/therapist, Ann, who probes my emotional landscape. Ann is a slender, middle-aged woman with short blonde hair, an easy manner, and a light touch. With her, there is no pretending that talking will make me feel better. I am good and well fucked. Why wouldn't I be a little off my game? She wants me to take a mood-elevating drug. Her desire to put me on the drug starts a debate. I stubbornly refuse to take any happy-time drug. She argues that it is just a very little dose. It will take some edge off what I am experiencing. She doesn't know I'm the stiff who wouldn't experiment with drugs, even when I was in Berkeley from 1965 to 1970, and it was the thing to do. Drugs were the key to a transformative cinema of the mind, so said the converts. I took a pass because I can't accept the idea of anything messing with my mind, which still seems plenty amazing straight from the factory. That is my intellectual reason. But I also fear loss of control, the very essence of the label "uptight." Ann wins the argument. She isn't peddling LSD or Prozac, and I can't tell how much downdraft my moods create; any uplift might help Jennifer, who stands in my weather system daily.

At the conference, Jennifer, Matt, and I are keyed up as we listen to the doctor make introductions. Up to this moment we've been on a roller coaster, reacting to what is in front of our noses. No one sat us down to give us the big picture. We've been filling that picture in with our fears. Dr. Skelza shows us an X-ray of my injury. He points to a place on the X-ray where a small fragment of bone pokes into my spinal cord at the C4 vertebra. It isn't a slasher stroke but a nudge. It's not much and too much at the same time. The not-much makes the injury incomplete. The too-much means the injury, even this poke, scrambles my system software and renders me a quadriplegic. If the poke had gone deeper, the cut and its scab would have blocked the cord, causing a complete injury, and my condition as a quadriplegic would have been permanent. Dr. Skelza explains that since my injury is incomplete, it is possible for me to regain function. How much is uncertain. More certain is that it will mostly happen in the two years following the accident. Craig plans to work with me for three months, their judgment of the time necessary to clear up my medical issues and test whether function will begin to show because of Caitlin's and Meghan's work. It is the time needed to prepare us to return home and teach Jennifer how to manage me as a quadriplegic. There is no high-beam flashing from Caitlin and Meghan today. Instead, everyone in the room is properly earnest and direct—this is the meeting to say how screwed Jim really is, and to lay out the options. They keep the focus on the work of therapy and seeing what will happen. I'm incomplete so I get to hope. They'll teach me the adaptations available to assist whatever function I do have. Every Friday they'll post a schedule on my door, showing the times each day for therapy or tech support or wheelchair adjustment or education.

Then Dr. Skelza asks for questions. Everyone looks at the three of us and waits. Jennifer is trying to take in all she's heard. She's still in processing-deficit mode. Matt wants to be sure I engage.

"Dad, don't you have a question?"

I blurt out, "Does this mean I'm going to croak sooner rather than later?"

I am pretty much a mess. I can't move, I'm on oxygen, I wear a catheter, my legs do the spasm dance, my blood is in the dumpster. I need a lift to move from bed to wheelchair, and help with dressing, bathing, eating, and taking a dump. As I speak, my voice trembles and I squeeze back tears. *Now* I cry. Let's hear it for New England restraint. The doctor calmly bats away my question, saying the length of my life won't be any different because of the injury. He can't calm the anxiety over the thought of death that merges with my body's roadside wreck. In my accident I'd experienced a death of who I was. I don't know how to talk about this. Jennifer and I have not begun to grieve this loss.

As my routine sets in I'm struck by how my condition resembles that of the fabled Eastern pasha. You know the picture. The sultan lying on tasseled cushions, fed grapes, fanned, all physical effort done by willing young women. My condition is not so dissimilar. This is how I rise in the morning. While still in bed, a voice solicits my wishes about what to wear. A young woman enters carrying a tray with my breakfast and my morning pills. A woman's hand feeds me, as I do nothing. My bedclothes are pulled back so I'm lounging naked in bed, discreetly covered by a small cloth. My wardrobe is presented. Pants slipped on, no underwear needed, then socks, then running shoes, a cruel joke. I'm enfolded in a version of a flying carpet, lifted in the air, and gently deposited in my magic chair. Once I am seated my assistant slips a shirt over my head. Every attention is given to adjusting my body to secure my comfort. My face is washed, my hair is combed. There is a flutter of attention over my posture, solicitous inquiries for anything more I might need, and they are gone. A real sultan peremptorily expects all will be done for him. I have no power to command this attention, only need. I fear that part of being a sultan is becoming a flaming asshole.

I leave this forced luxury to take on the role of a supplicant, where others put me to work, help me, feed me, teach me, and love me. Being a supplicant is foreign territory; I have to ask for help where I never did before. Asking for help has never been a habit for me, unless I am in deep shit. Surely this qualifies, as I'm learning how to reclaim my independence. At the end of the day I return to my room, where I'll be gathered up and taken for a bath. This part of the day is very not like a sultan's. It's more like being a worker on a space freighter on course to some distant mining planet. My keepers arrive, pluck me from my chair, set me in a wheeled industrial contraption, and bring me to a washing facility so they can hose me down, clean me, shave me, dry me off, and bring me to my sleeping cubicle. Sleep is induced with the aid of pharmaceuticals. Then, like a drone, I'm stashed in a work cubby until needed in the morning.

Something that I look forward to does happen when I am wheeled off for my bath. I have every reason to disengage from those constantly handling my body, always reminding me of my helplessness. I do just the opposite. For the bath I am taken to a shower room that serves my ward, replete with institutional tile, a towel supply closet, and the look of heavy use. What happens is that I cannot help wanting to talk to the young women who come to ready me for my time in the shower room. I want to know who they are and what they believe. After all, this is an intimate business. I'm helpless and naked in a rolling chair, and their task is to scrub me down head to toe and conduct the even more intimate daily bowel ritual. They are young women who could be my daughters by age. There is one petite young woman with short black hair who has the look of "I've navigated more borders than you." She looks like the person you want to ask if you don't know where the hell you are or whom to trust. She is alert and alive and enjoys her expertise at making me comfortable. She is from Romania and came to America by herself. She arrived with no support system but her own wits and desire. She describes how her friends in Romania fear to leave, to break loose from the ruts and the compromises they've made to accept a life with few options.

Seeing my age, she cautiously asks, "Who do you want to win the election?"

"Obama," I say immediately.

She ducks her face and grins. "Yes, I like him very much."

Even though it is just my head in the game, our talk makes me feel like myself. I've spent my life around young people as a university teacher. Seeing her earned toughness and savoir faire is as good as a drug. Another night it is a tall girl with tattoos up and down her arms. Boots, tights, cut-off jeans, dyed slash of hair, the full hipster. She has a no-holds-barred laugh that I work to release. They welcome my engagement. Vicariously touching their vitality is a much needed piece of evidence that my own is not lost.

Remember, I can now talk. After surgery and my time in the University of New Mexico Hospital ICU, the trachea tube hole at the base of my throat left me speechless. It was a shock to be made silent. As a dean I spent my days talking in meetings, lunching with donors, cajoling chairs to work on this or that issue, making speeches, panhandling the provost, talking the occasional outraged faculty member out of a tree, selling the college like a hot car, and being a cheerleader socializer. Add to that my private life with Jennifer, our children, our friends, and my chance to rant about politics and fill my America balloon with the air of purple mountains and fruited plains. Add also the ever-present popsicle stand of gossip that's always open on a university campus. That's a lot to lose in a three-foot fall. My silence meant Jennifer and I could not speak to each other about what all this means or how we feel. At Craig they adjusted my trachea with a valve that allows enough air for my voice box to sound. Do we even want to wade into these feelings? Without saying so out loud, we fear we might drown.

I get off the oxygen machine in record time, or so I think after all the congrats I receive. Another speedy business is the disappearance of my feeding tube. It happens as an accident. One of the techs makes a mistake and partly pulls it out when transferring me from chair to bed. First they try to reinsert it because they don't know if I can eat enough calories to maintain my energy level for the work I need to do in my therapy sessions. It takes three tries to stick it back down my nose to my stomach. Failing on the first two tries, they use a smaller tube and slip the last attempt all the way to home base. You can imagine how great it feels to have a plastic tube stuck down your nose and throat. To be sure it is actually in my stomach correctly, they take an X-ray. It isn't. They slide it out, making my insides go wobbly, and throw in the towel. I'm free to eat solid food. Breathing on my own, eating, and talking, I feel ready for the Wheaties box. After a bow to luck and know-how, score a point towards walking two miles every morning with Jennifer and our dogs.

Free to eat, but unable to feed myself, I have to banish images of the old and feeble being fed gruel in a Dickensian world. The cafeteria is in the same room used for daily therapy: tables are put up and down when needed. If I want to eat and Jennifer is busy, I have to find a "grub

buddy." They are staff members from different depart-
ments in the hospital. They stand near the food counter waiting for someone to catch their eye. Forget the
sway of being the dean of a college, managing budgets
and personnel and strategic plans. Instead, start looking
for a stranger who will take my order, fetch my lunch,
then hand-feed it to me. Surprisingly, instead of feeling
ashamed at being spoon-fed, I use it (like bath time) as
a chance to socialize, a way to practice a normality that
is ripped to shreds and needs reinvention. Although it is
not the local lunch hot spot full of the bustle of mating
display and career gossip, I have company.

The Craig routine usually begins at nine o'clock. I
have to be awake, dressed, fed, and medicated before I
drive my chair to work in the therapy room. Before it is
light, a tech appears beside my bed, sticks me with a needle, and sucks out some blood, then pokes a needle in my
stomach to ward off blood clots. The vampire draw was
for a doctor assigned to Geritol my blood. I always have
Caitlin and Meghan for therapy. There is manipulating
and stretching and testing and lots of talking at first to
create a baseline from which they can measure change.
Right off there is laughing, one of the best ingredients in
their therapy recipes. I spend the day shifting from session to session, then have lunch with Jennifer or a grub
buddy. I have a session with the counselor, Ann. She is
trying to figure out my narrative. Am I the story of the
listless boy on the bridge staring into the river below?
Am I the story of the boy stuck in a snowbank, ready
to dig out with his bare hands despite the cold? Or am I
the story of the boy who puts on a brave face to hide his
fear? She knows I come from Yankee snow country and
has to decide if I am any or none of the above depending on the day. Some days I have a session in the educa-

tion room. An amazingly tough and savvy woman, herself in a wheelchair, dispenses spiritual and practical talk, steering us away from the "Why did this happen?" to the "What can we do?" I may have a session in the activity room where they encourage me to pursue a hobby, do crafts, and sign up for an outing. Except for outings, this makes me get-off-my-damn-lawn-you-f-ing-kids angry. It is irrational. Wheelchairs pulled up to craft tables make me want to scream, make me think of geezer world and nursing homes. The young woman running the place is very tolerant and lets me have my fit without taking offense. The rest of my schedule is a tonic. I am doing something, being active, generating hope that this is going to lead somewhere. Weekend schedules are blank, the time our own.

Jennifer begins making her own routine to keep her sanity. She discovers the gym and the daily workout classes for staff that she can join. At home she thrives on a busy life. Her exile with me at Craig has subtracted so much from her world that she instinctively finds ways to complicate the simplicity. Before, when we headed off to do something together, she might forget a hat or a sweater. I would be out the door going about our business and she would catch up. Now, there is no such thing as my going out the door and getting on with it. Now when we start off, I notice she creates a new way of gathering the things she needs. She might need her iPad, some piece of information, her iPhone, her glasses—and all the objects will be in different places. Instead of planning a single trip, going place-to-place to collect all her strayed items, she unconsciously creates a serial adventure by retrieving one item, returning, then thinking of something else she needs, and immediately walking away to find it. Or, when we are about to embark on some project together, she might think of a question for the nurse that could be asked later, but she will bolt off to fetch her answer. It's for me to keep my mouth shut; these actions fit her need as a fierce spirit in motion making the most of her new limits.

The second or third Saturday of our stay, Jennifer and I find a small, pleasant room with carpet, chairs, and a window where patients and visitors meet. It is empty. We go in and, without saying much, I begin to cry. I can talk, but I can't. I really don't know what words to use. It isn't the kind of crying that is a release; it is a kind of weeping over something inexplicable. It feels like the news of death but it isn't death. Everything has changed. We don't want to say it. It is terrible in a way I don't want to talk about. She holds me. She cries, just as lost as I am for what to say. This is not the time to say, "Everything will be all right." We avoid brave gestures about the future. We don't feel brave. There is something about our speechless state that is true. We are angry, but find it ridiculous to yell or break something. We are also perfectly reasonable. Something has been taken. It isn't like us to just lie down because of it. We are in a rowboat drifting out of sight of the shore. Where will we wash up?

In a scene from Mike Leigh's film *Topsy-Turvy*, the actress Shirley Henderson sits in her dressing room and gazes rapturously at herself in a mirror just before she goes onstage to sing "The Sun, Whose Rays Are All Ablaze" as Yum-Yum in *The Mikado*. She wonders who can be more beautiful than she. Assured there is none, she asks herself what's the cause? Is it vanity? No, it's nature. It's nature without thought, reason, money in the bank, or crimes on the ledger that doles out beauty, pain, joy, ugliness, catastrophe, and wonder. If, however, we do treat her claim of beauty as vanity, then we have to treat it as an item on a moral ledger: she deserves what happens, here's the reason, here's the moment, here's the crime, she'll do the time. If we agree she is beautiful and it's just profligate nature that made her so, then life has no prescribed plan, no fate logged in the heavens. We are all alone with our choices, our will, our fear, our desire, and our curiosity to see what nature offers. There is no scorekeeper, only the chance to seize what experience brings, grow from its beauty and brace for its cruelty. Does that mean we don't suffer? What's to prevent it? Even in suffering we can see the sun, whose rays are all ablaze.

Suffering was neither weakness nor pitiable agony for the Greeks. In the tragedies, the experience depicts a self-knowledge that is astounding, terrible; in their stories it connects the highest born to the lowest, it makes a democracy of life's catastrophes and value. This isn't Mother Teresa's idea of suffering, a suffering where the more real the pain felt by the sick and dying, the greater its value, as if kissed by Jesus. The Greeks don't value the agony and pain; they value the changed life that comes because of it. Electra in Sophocles's play is a warrior of suffering. Listening to her you become exhausted by the force expelled in her expression of her life's catastrophe— sister sacrificed, mother in bed with a hated lover, father murdered in his bath at the hand of his wife. Dreaming of revenge, she is consumed with misery and fury. She is a cautionary figure of tragedy adrift with hate. Her story ends in chaos and blood.

Heracles is a different story. He returns home at the peak of his triumphs, the completion of his labors, and is driven mad by a god. When he enters his home, a terrible delusion forms in his mind, causing him to see his wife and children as beasts. He hunts them with bow and arrow until he slays each one. After he recovers his mind he recognizes what he's done. He is no longer the Heracles of his labors. He is Heracles the man: broken, lost.

Euripides does not shame or judge him. Theseus, ruler of Athens, comes to help Heracles, and finds him after his madness, hiding his face in shame. Heracles tells him to flee: he is unfit, diseased. Theseus answers, "Where there is love contagion cannot come." When Heracles relents to go with Theseus and accept his shelter, he speaks to his need to face suffering:

> Even in misery I asked myself,
> Would it not be cowardice to die?
> The man who cannot bear up under fate
> Could never face the weapons of man.
> I shall prevail against death. I shall go to your city.

Heracles is led away by the sympathetic Theseus to sanctuary in Athens. Euripides shows a man changed, but present to live with what he's done.

> I, whose whole house has gone down in grief,
> Am towed in Theseus's wake like some little boat.
> The man who would prefer great wealth or strength
> More than love, more than friends, is diseased of soul.

For me this insight—how life is both broken and sustained in the suffering that animates Greek tragedy—is freeing. Suffering calls for recognition and acceptance, not shame or despair.

THE GLASS-COVERED BRIDGE between the two wings of the hospital is usually bathed in sun. Patients maneuver themselves like lizards to this place to look out at the mountains and to feel the heat. The weekend after we allow ourselves to cry together, we come to this bridge. Jennifer sits on a low ledge that runs along the edge of the glass wall. Her iPad is in her lap. I want to write down what is happening to me, perhaps because when we wept, foreheads pressed together, there were no words. I have to find words. The act of journaling becomes a need I fill each week. It is a discipline, an excuse to knock on the door that slammed shut when I fell. Can I find the person I was when every moment shoves what I'm not in my face? Written language is one of the few things I can control, even though I require help with the act. I dictate to Jennifer. This feels like being in the game, even though I don't know what the game is. I won't hide under a rock to brood and withdraw. I have reason to. Why not?

I started keeping a journal in college, taken by the act of thinking that appears like an unkempt dog found crouched under one's bed. I was seduced by complexity and abstraction, head-in-the-clouds seriousness and that New England constraint of emotion sticking to me like musk. My journaling exhibits how I sort myself out by writing it down. I haven't yet asked myself, "What does it mean to be paralyzed? What do I feel?" I hold these questions away, trying to go through each day avoiding them. I am like a child who won't say "I want a new bike" out loud. Saying it will jinx the chance that the wish will become real on his birthday. Don't say "paralyzed," don't jinx return of movement. Like fingering worry beads, I go from thing to thing each day, focused on the pleasant and unpleasant until I can reach sleep and oblivion. Other than Jennifer, the only person who tries to lift the rock on my emotions is Ann, who asks how I feel each time we meet. To answer, I do a version of windmilling my arms and dancing backward, claiming I am fine.

I am not rending my garments and cursing the heavens. I perch on a thin ledge of objectivity: a random accident carries no special meaning. I will not indulge in "Why me?" See, my hand is not shaking; there are no cuts on my wrist.

I talk and Jennifer types. It is a chance for her to hear my thoughts. It is hard for a woman of constant motion to be tied to my circumscribed world. She is a wonderful cook. She quickly seizes on dinner as something that she'll do. No cafeteria trays brought by the nurse. It is a reason to go shopping. It is a reason to think about something approaching normal. Each night, she brings dinner to my room. What is not normal is that I can't feed myself. She is a proud cook, even under these conditions, and it bothers her that I can't taste her meals because of the medicines. After dinner a tech comes to fetch me for my daily bath and bowel routine. When I disappear, Jennifer takes away the dishes. She comes back when I am stuck in bed. She flosses my teeth and kisses me good night. Sometimes she says good night when the tech shows up. It is too hard to come back. There are days she looks like a ghost of herself. I am not giving off much emotional wattage. She is basically alone. The writing makes a place where she can have something of me.

I'm not looking in the mirror struck by how beautiful I am. But I am glad to embrace nature which, in her excess, blind though she is, gives up beauty and catastrophe, butterflies and sharks, sow bugs and great oaks. And it is nature's will to blaze so. Yum-Yum sings:

> The sun, whose rays
> Are all ablaze
> With ever-living glory,
> Does not deny

His majesty—
He scorns to tell a story!
He don't exclaim,
"I blush for shame,
So kindly be indulgent."
But, fierce and bold,
In fiery gold,
He glories all effulgent!
I mean to rule the earth,
As he the sky—
We really know our worth,
The sun and I!

CHAPTER TWO

Spineless

HOW AM I LIKE Darwin's fish which, driven by hunger, leaves the water to walk on its fins over mud after bugs? When it grows a brain and legs and lives in America, will it learn the difference between lurching after bugs and civility?

The glass bridge where I began my journal separates the medical ward from the prepare-to-go-home ward. To cross it, I have to be free of my medical issues. The glass bridge is where we creatures collect, tilt back, and show our bellies to the sun. I can shrug both shoulders. I have some motion in my left arm, and more in my right. Caitlin is working on them. She schedules me for e-stim (electrical stimulation) work, where electrodes are placed on a particular muscle to direct an electric current, causing the muscle to contract. With my arms wired, I try to rotate a wheel with a handle on each side, like pedals on a bicycle wheel. They decide my shoulder is too messed up to continue this exercise. I can lift my right wrist almost to my lips. A little forward head nod is required to close the deal. I'm tasked with stabbing a piece of food and lifting it to my mouth. I make it, but if I have to rely on this skill to eat, I'll starve.

Meghan is focused on waking up my legs. She uses various stretches. She cranes me onto a low platform, where she manipulates my legs. I try to stay awake and not kick her onto the floor with a spasm. A dangling carrot in my routine is the therapy pool, a prize on hold until the hole from my now-removed trachea tube heals closed.

Caitlin and Meghan adopt Jennifer as their stealth therapist during my off hours. Jennifer comes to many of my sessions and watches what they do. For me, half of the therapy is talking and joking with these young women while they mess with my body. Caitlin has an easy and infectious laugh, and I enjoy trying to make her crack up. At first she is easily freaked by my grimaces, but then learns not to cut me any slack as she counts repetitions and stretches an arm. Working with Meghan is equally fun, but different. She loves thinking up new ways of trying to get me in motion, so I never know which Meghan will show up to our session. Will it be the serious girl who's going to stick to the usual PT routines, or the wild girl who'll say, "Let's do some crazy shit today and see what happens"? Safe Meghan keeps me on the mat, manipulating and stretching me. Wild Megan tries standing me up, held by the lift device as she moves my feet to see what I can do, as I think, "I'm not nearly ready! What are you doing?" Meghan taps into some instinct in me that wants to break the rules and go past my fear of the activities she wants me to do. Jennifer sits nearby with her iPad until she can't stand being still any longer. Then she shoots away for an errand or goes to the gym. Caitlin and Meghan know Jennifer will work on me later using some of the exercises they take me through, ones I can do in my chair. When I'm alone with Jennifer, there is no joking to release me from the grip of her focus on the task at hand. Sympathy, yes, but no escape by playing the "Oh, you poor baby" card.

The other inmates on the glass bridge are soaking up the sun, but Jennifer is beside me, either stretching something or counting as I strain to lift one arm or my shoulders while she patiently counts repetitions and tells me to lift, go higher. When I strain to raise my hand to my mouth or stretch farther, these therapists, including the stealthy one, always tell me to go further. I answer with the unforgivable, "I can't." I get a look as if I had just insulted God, the flag, and the Constitution. I protest that I've been kidnapped by a terrorist cell of positive thinkers. They ha, ha, ha, but keep the steely look in their eyes.

An example of progress: I have a beeper attached to my chair. It goes off every fifteen minutes, reminding me to press a button that tilts the chair so my feet come up and I'm resting on my back. I stay for three minutes, the beeper sounds again, and I press the button to return to a sitting position. I do this to take weight off my butt to prevent sores. The button was rigged at the side of my headrest so I could press it with the side of my head, which was the only part of me strong enough for the job. Now the button is rigged beside my right armrest, because my right hand is strong enough to keep it pushed in until the chair finishes its tilt up and down. Pathetic, no? Still, I'll bow to the overwhelmed and undervalued god of small progress.

This is what I understand now about my spine and how it heals. The therapies that manipulate and exercise my body and strengthen the muscles are a kind of temple dancing. It is temple dancing because we have faith that the god of the spinal cord will decide to return and fully inhabit my body. It is an invocation, a practice of patience because doctors don't know a way to direct the nerve messages around the injury site to my muscles. Time is now a new medium in which I float. I've always had patience, but this is different. I look at it as a kind of cosmic magic. I think of the world as a profound mystery, so my injury gives a new reality and new stakes to my belief.

Matt comes to visit. He brings his camera. He plans to film every twitch of my existence here, all the action on the various gizmos I use in therapy: "My Dad, the Quadro." He coaches me on my cell phone and computer and shows me his techno savvy. He's a filmmaker, so it's no surprise he's a tech savant. He prods me to download the dictation program called Dragon. I'd been putting it off—too this, too that, the usual sorry BS. Dragon can open other programs and dictate in any text window, even e-mail. We play with it just enough to see that it has an impressive capacity and a serious learning curve. Craig gives tutorials on the program. It is a pleasure to realize that I will not have to shut up if I cannot operate my keyboard or if Jennifer has an actual life besides taking my dictation.

With Matt, hip LA is in the building. The shoes, the cool pants, and the stubble beard. He's in the scene—no muss, no fuss, but you know it's there. He's carrying a compact hi-def camera he operates as if it were as simple as an old Brownie. If we stand next to each other, he is slightly shorter, his frame neither thick nor thin, but compact and athletic, reflecting the competitive snowboarder he once was. Normally we talk politics, movies, and what's happening in his career and family. On this visit he has to slow down his brain, which races like a train, and take in his father, altered and hurt. He becomes a cheerleader and a coach, treating me like an athlete in an elite training camp. He works his charm and confidence into me like liniment. His camera normalizes me, as if I'm this interesting thing that's not broken, but unusual. He takes Jennifer to dinner, releasing pressure, reanimating the touch and feel of family, and banishing for a moment the world of the hospital. He's a talker, a nourishing drink for us both.

WHY DID DESCARTES spend his thinking and writing time in bed? It draws attention to the furious action of his mind while his body is set aside. How does one use or need the other? I send my weekly journaling to my family and my secretary at the university, so she can share it with my colleagues in the office. Close colleagues write to say they think my reports show that my spirit is back. How do they know? Great, my spirit is back; where is that spirit located? My body module is adrift and has lost communication with my mind-ship, which is orbiting alone. My mind spends its days sending communiqués to my body, but fails to connect. The difference between these parts of myself was always complicated or unspoken, even without an injury. What is that thing below my neck? My body creates spasms, it drops like dead weight, shows glimmers of movement in response to my commands, and rebels because it can't, not won't, accede to my requests. But it is a two-way street. There is no "I'll pick up my marbles and move to Fresno" by either half of this couple. What are the consequences of the civil war going on between my halves?

My right wrist shows new movement. I touch my thumb to my forefinger. When Matt shows me how to work my Bluetooth earpiece, he says, "Dad, touch your ear." I do. It surprises the hell out of me. I didn't believe my arm could make that move. It gives me as much pleasure as a toddler eating his toes. It is like my mind grew a new finger. It isn't like answering a general's orders; it is a companionship. I don't pretend I'm smart enough to philosophize with Descartes. I am relearning about mind and body in a way that is maddening and daunting. When some new companionship happens, I want it all to return instantly. The body says, "Not so fast, Jocko, you've got to take the ride." Neither mind nor body is fully in control of how and where it goes.

After almost four weeks the Craig staff is ready to move me across the glass bridge to the east wing, where I'll share my room with Jennifer. We will begin learning how to live on our own. She will move out of the apartment and into my room, a kind of playing house where she is expected to learn the routines of managing my body. Crossing the bridge means I have no more medical issues. I am just a quadriplegic who has to be managed. We are not ready. We don't want to start thinking about being home and leaving behind all the support at Craig. I'm easily spooked by the unfamiliar. I fear inexperienced, less-skilled staff. I tense when someone new shows up to handle my bathing routine. If I gain more function, Craig might extend my stay to work on those new abilities to see what more they can get out of them. I have relentless coaching, but it's frustrating to shoot blanks into my body, asking it to move. I carve out a space where I don't allow myself to focus on my overall lack of function. Most of my day is taken up with the work of keeping my head glued on straight—pretending to know what that is.

Children ask to have things done for them that they can do themselves. They whine with impatience, indulge in martyred gestures and tones of voice, and bark with frustration and anger. None of this is sustainable in a relationship, especially where one is able and one is not. Some husband I am. My sense of touch is as though I have thick felt covering the skin of my hands. I have a catheter in my dick and can't show how happy I am to see her. If she touches or hugs me, I spasm. If we go for a walk I whir alongside in a small vehicle that weighs several hundred pounds. You don't want me anywhere near your feet. I am a complete baby, afraid of new terrain and obsessed with my body and my need to feel safe. This is when the line in the vow—"in sickness and in health"—is tested, that's for fucking sure.

But I am there somewhere, the familiar face and voice. I am learning a new discipline of talking without drama about our new reality. It is like a play. It takes rehearsal. It doesn't always work. We both cling to a belief that this will change, though we don't know how. I am an absence that is yet to be defined. I am in some in-between state, a ghost amid the overwhelming demands of the present. My assigned mystery is how to coax muscles to fire and renew connections between us.

By design, the culture here is relentlessly positive. Just do it; if not, we'll teach you how to manage without it. We will make this work. We aren't giving up and neither can you. It is hard to imagine the blind Oedipus, wandering in exile with his daughters, encountering this culture. Before he knew it, he would be outfitted with a cane, enrolled in a support group, have his diet checked and improved, and be given books on tape about living a full life. But suffering is everywhere, like water vapor. Suffering marks us all, it just isn't clear what it will do to each of us.

This is most visible at lunch. I always take breakfast in my room, and Jennifer's need to do something, create some routine of connection with me that is remotely

normal, creates supper. But at lunch we gather like exotic
creatures at a waterhole. Bodies of different sizes and
ages, thick and thin, held in their powered contraptions.
Each chair has something to personalize it: a knapsack, a
sticker, a gizmo to hold a cell phone, a tricked-out water
bottle in a holder, or a soft canteen and drinking tube;
some have oxygen.

Arrayed around the tables, everyone wears some kind
of athletic shoes and loose-fitting pants and jersey tops,
clothing that is easy to put on and suitable for working
with the therapists. We all have water bottles attached to
our chairs so we can hydrate for the health of our blad-
ders, and everyone is catheterized, with capture bags
strapped to our legs. There is an older man here because
of a virus gone rogue, his wife by his side. A kid is here
because of a gunshot wound. A younger man, a hunter
who always dresses in camouflage, was injured when he
fell off his blind platform. He lay face down, arms pinned
under him, for thirteen hours before he was found.
There is the father who souped up a go-cart for his kids
and had a terrible wreck on a trial run. Then there's the
snowmobiler who flipped over. His accident has made his
house in the mountains inaccessible. There is a young
man, a bicyclist, who rode behind a trash truck. He didn't
notice when the truck stopped further ahead, right in his
path. His head was down; he pedaled to pick up speed and
smashed into the truck head-on. He is paralyzed from the
waist down. Some patients move their chairs with hand
controls and some move by puffing into a plastic tube,
controlling their direction and speed with breath. Except for the bicyclist, all are quadriplegic. All have somebody with them, except for a contractor from Texas and
one younger woman. She will return home to manage
her new needs alone.

We are at Craig at the same time, so it feels like a class in school. We observe each other's mental state and severity of injury. There is the obligatory question in every first meeting: "What happened?" I talk with the contractor from Texas, who fell at a job site. He struggles to find food that doesn't make him sick. He is here alone because he has children and his wife works. There is a farmer from Wyoming, closer to my age, who is nearly ready to graduate and go home. We talk about the drought that is changing his region, with no relief in sight. He can't accept that climate change could be the cause. We are all tended by helpers who feed us as we bob up and down, using the tilt buttons on our chairs to prevent butt sores. We look like a collection of toy birds that kids put on the rim of a glass to watch them dip in and out of the water.

The food is what you'd find at an old neighborhood diner: casseroles your grandmother made, always fixings for salad, chicken, fish, and meat in some version recognizable from a bygone era when men wore fedoras and women wore stockings. For me, every meal is the story of how my right arm is not in the game. I need to borrow someone's arm and hand to put food in my mouth. "Oh, you can move your arm!" Yeah, about halfway up my chest. Can I lift it high enough to hoist a fork over my miserable neck brace and take a bite? This movie has a simple soundtrack: "Almost, almost, a little bit more, holy fucking shit useless son of a bitch miserable stinking pile of crap asshole, wake up, wake up, do your goddamned job." Well, that feels better. I am not an in-the-flow, calm, visualize-and-execute kind of guy.

The room is noisy with talk, the clatter of dishes in the cafeteria line, the comings and goings of nurses picking up food for patients who can't leave their rooms, and

staff who cycle through an auxiliary kitchen to micro-
wave their lunches. The talk is as useful as the food. The
bustle is purposeful, as we have to finish by one o'clock
when the cafeteria disappears and, without missing a
beat, becomes a therapy room again.

Suffering is a constant companion, an amoral antagonist that shapes and colors every aspect of our experience once we are in its grip. Endurance will dress our
suffering in the costume of a donkey, a plodding beast of
burden. It is easy to think that suffering means enduring
misfortune and pain, whether of the body or the heart.
But suffering is not a grief that sweeps us away and dis-
cards us, diminished, on a rocky shore, where we get up,
bent, with a weight on our heart. It is a part of how we
learn to know ourselves again after we are lost. This is
true, but it's not the whole meaning. There are times
when these words are just spin that belong on the noble
dung heap of sentiment, when suffering is a psycho dog
chained to your ankle, alternately licking your hand and
trying to tear your heart out.

Before my pitch off the porch, Jennifer and I found
ways to connect to each other despite the ongoing pres-
sures of love and work. When I was department chair,
Jennifer began to choreograph dances that use text. There
is a writer she knows sleeping in her bed. For me it is a
smack to the back of my head: stop whining about the
budget, write something. Rehearsal might not be an
aphrodisiac, but it put us in each other's pockets. The
rest we can work out. As we brush our teeth together one
night, she looks at me in the mirror with an I-have-news
expression. "Guess who is invited to Israel to a dance fes-
tival? I can bring two pieces. I have one; write me something for the other. You can earn your way." Our bed is
bookended by our two black Labs, oblivious as we slip

under the covers. I say, "OK, I'll write something for you, but it'll cost you extra." I roll against her to negotiate payment.

It's been two months since the disaster near a Mexican beach. The space between our two bodies, so simply made intimate by rolling on my side, is a physical gulf, my arms without reach or sensation of touch. The trip to Israel we took then is now a fantastical thought. I wrote a short script she used with her choreography. It was centered on a choral passage in a Greek tragedy, something that stuck in my head when I heard it sung in Lee Breuer's production of *The Gospel at Colonus*. The choral ode stayed with me like a beautiful stone found on a beach beside the desiccated body of a great creature from the deep. It remained a cautionary find, something to touch at the start of each day. It is one of Sophocles's great choral odes. Breuer lifts it from *Antigone* for *The Gospel at Colonus*, an African American musical version of Sophocles's *Oedipus at Colonus*. The ode is an anthem to human majesty and fragility. In *Antigone*, Oedipus's two sons, Eteocles and Polynices, inherit the throne after he is exiled. Cursed by their father, they fight over the prize. Polynices gathers an army and is killed when he attacks Thebes to seize the prize for himself. Creon, who assumes the throne, decrees that the usurper's body remain unburied, left to the dogs and vultures. Death will be the consequence for anyone who defies this order. Sophocles places the choral ode, like an expansion joint, between two events: the moment a guard arrives, fearing to tell Creon that someone has buried Polynices, and the moment he reveals that Polynices was buried by the cursed man's sister, tragic Oedipus's daughter/sister Antigone. Hers is the old, irrepressible story: the individual who blazes defiant against authority. Why does Sophocles have the chorus summon up an elegiac description of humanity between these moments? The chorus tells us of the one thing that makes our human mastery an illusion.

Numberless Are the Days

I can't remember the teacher who made me memorize an ode from Sophocles or why she thought it was important. I can barely remember the name of the school or the town I come from. I remember the color of the book—green. I sit at the top of the stairs in my pajamas, reading. I don't answer anyone who speaks to me. I sit there, mumbling the words over and over. My eyes trace the repeated pattern in the rug rising up the stairs, hoping it holds a spell to make the words rise from the page and take root in my brain. My brother creeps up behind me and whispers, "Are you retarded? I know you don't really belong in this family. You know why? Dad was too embarrassed to take you back as a mistake." I shut my eyes and recite:

> Numberless are the world's wonders
> But none more wonderful than man
> Storm gray seas yield to his prows
> The huge crests bear him high
> Earth holy and inexhaustible is
> Graven with shining furrows
> Where his plows have gone year after year
> The timeless labor of stallions.

It happened again, doctor. I couldn't sleep. That dream returned last night! What? Do I have to? Of course I'll sit down. Here? I'm sorry. I'm just in a hurry to tell you. In the dream I'm standing . . . I'm standing on a street. I don't recognize anything. I'm lost . . . I'm afraid. I try to find something familiar . . . someone I know. A mother screams at her child in the next building. Children . . . are everywhere. They run up and down the streets. They are frantic. They are scrounging in vacant lots for stones and trash to make a barricade in the street. In the distance I hear the voices of men arguing and yelling, coming closer. The children look at me . . . they want me to finish the barricade. The sound grows louder . . . nearer. I see a stone at my feet, but I have no strength to lift it. I squeeze my eyes shut and recite:

> Man, the light boned birds and beasts that cling to cover
> The lithe fish lighting their reaches of dim water
> All are taken and tamed in the net of his mind.

Sure I do. Stop. But it's just that I . . . Are the kids asleep? Well you know. I . . . we are . . . we have . . . we need to . . . ah . . . change. Did you say why? You know, I thought we had something. Have something. You can't tell? What do you mean? So you want to, you can . . . throw it away? Still, what about the children? We need . . . to tell them. Sure I know . . . I'm not blind. Why would I? It's true. Yes, when? Wait, do you . . . Do you know what you're doing?

> The lion on the hill
> The wild horse, windy maned resigns to him
> And his blunt yoke
> Has broken the sultry shoulders of the mountain bull.

Wait. Hey, keep it down. Listen! I'm on the phone. Leave her alone . . . I'm being perfectly clear. Hold on . . . Go to your own room. Now . . . Like I said, I've done all I'm going to. No! You went out the fucking door? You know why. I can't say it again. What? I owe you? Dream

on. Oh, you don't think I'm what? I can't hear you. Am I
what? . . . Happy?

I close my eyes.

> Man, words also and thoughts as rapid as air
> He fashions to his good use
> Statecraft is his and his skill that
> Deflects the arrows of snow
> The spears of winter rain
> From every wind he has made himself secure

Goodnight, Dad. No, I won't stay up too late. Dad, wait.
I don't understand this part? Will you . . . and Mom . . . ?

> From every wind he has made himself secure
> From all but one
> In the late wind of death
> He cannot stand.

I can't separate my response to this ode from the way
it's used in Lee Breuer's *The Gospel at Colonus*. The production is framed as a sermon in a black church. The
action takes place before a huge African American gospel choir. Oedipus enters in a white suit, played by one
of the singers in the group called The Five Blind Boys of
Alabama. Oedipus comes to Colonus to die. His suffering has made him a figure of spiritual value. In the play,
Oedipus's death is mysterious and unseen by the chorus. Sophocles makes death into a restorative event for
the tragic Oedipus. In Breuer's production, after Oedipus dies, he returns, rising from below playing a white
piano while the choir sings a standing, hand-clapping,
roof-raising gospel hymn with the refrain, "Lift him up!"
I take up this image with its raw vitality that undoes the
meaning of death and puts in motion the singing body,
fierce with joy, as a lever to pry up the phrase, "He can-

not stand." I place this image in the front row next to my inner skeptic with bed hair, fixed by crumpled will and scorn for hope. His "I can'ts" are companion to the efforts to move my body, the therapies, the stretches, the "go highers," the transfers, the spasms, and all that brings pain.

A continuing part of my awareness is how to tolerate degrees of pain. The pain is not constant. For me, pain happens during movement, when working in therapy. Some is caused by the sensitivity of my frozen left shoulder, and some is gritchy-yowly feelings in my joints and muscles, as if I were a rusted tin man. A hand brushing over the surface of my skin can set off a strong spasm. If I'm still and don't have spasms, I'm OK. But my body can't be still. I'm a groaner, a noisemaker when I strain, lift, or push, like the tennis pros. I'm a grimace monkey. I have a whole range of faces I make depending on the degree of pain I anticipate. I can be stoic about pain, but it is new to have pain as part of what I do every day. If I take a pill or medical cannabis for it, I'm making a trade for zombiehood. My pain is something that attaches to me like the way I walk or the way I dress. There are several times a day when I clench my teeth and bang on the arm of my chair with my good arm. What does this get me? Not much. The pain is at a level of "suck it up and gut it out." It is related to the activity of the moment: once the activity stops, the pain quits. The scale ranges from yell-out-loud "Stop," to cursing when I get rolled on my bad shoulder, to the exquisite pain of therapy stretches on this shoulder or enduring a spasm that won't give up. Jennifer is a true expert in this arena, as are all professional dancers. Too much empathy is of no help. Jennifer considers pain a natural by-product of exercise. She works with me with the dancer's practiced demeanor: "You can get through this; you're a big boy." That's questionable. In my condition, I'm not a big boy. I want to say, "Fuck the challenge." This is when getting my right arm to open the door to my room is a ridiculous victory. It is the time when I'm anxious about going on an elevator alone, as it is very hard to reach and push the buttons. But, not so long ago, I couldn't manage the buttons at all.

When Jennifer pauses from making supper in our room or from working on her email, her attention sweeps over me like NORAD (North American Aerospace Defense). This sets in motion more challenges: pick up peanuts with the fingers of my working hand, put my forearm against the wall and push against it, try to reach higher. She arranges a test course of peanuts, corn nuts, cheese pieces, and carrots for me to pick up and move to my mouth. Early in this minuet her radar finds me daydreaming. She hands me a ball of sticky putty to squeeze and runs off to check our laundry. I am alone with my sticky putty. My grip is weak and it falls out of my hand onto my lap. It is one thing to squeeze a ball of putty, quite another to pick it up from my lap. Sticky putty left on a surface melts. It spreads over my shirt and pants. The nurse comes in with pills and sees a giant yellow puddle in my lap. She asks, "Are you all right?" No, Mary Poppins, I'm not. I've taken many risks in my emotional and work life. This is different, a fight against myself, against the eternal sirens' song to do nothing.

Nothing I do in therapy, except for saying "I can't," is ever judged. They push, they teach me, and we share stories. I laugh as much as I grimace and struggle. The talk is as useful as the physical work because I am drawn out of any hole I might sink in and I relearn the need for connection. One day, Caitlin meets me for lunch to work on my eating technique. I know she is planning a wedding in a few months. She rigs up a device with counterweights to help me lift my hand to my lips. I strain to put food in my mouth. The gap is the width of my neck brace. My hand is the marshmallow recruit trying to climb the cargo-net barrier, except it's inches, and I fall back. The counterweight compensates for this last hurdle, boosting my hand over the neck brace to my mouth. Each lift is so hard that, in frustration, I ask her about her fiancé, hoping for anything but the maddening swoon of my hand. She allows a rest and tells me how she skipped any mother-daughter cooking lessons. She invited The One to come to her apartment for dinner. The headline is: Uh Oh, First Time Girlfriend Cooks for Boyfriend. Her plan is to cook a steak. How hard can that be? Except she'd never done it, nor seen one cooked. Meat wasn't a frequent meal in her mother's kitchen. The problem is too simple for Google, it's common sense—she reasons that if you boil an egg in water, why not a steak? Table set, pot of water ready on the stove, steak in the fridge; she's got it covered. He arrives. They have some drinks and some talk. His stomach rumbles, so in goes steak to boiling pot of water. Out comes the steak as gray and tough as the sole of a boot. Luckily the path to his heart is not through his stomach. My rest time is over. She says, "Lift, you're almost there." Afterward, I remember the laughs more than the pain and frustration.

The room where I work with Meghan and Caitlin is large, filled with low, padded mat tables, rolling work tables, cupboards full of equipment, and a walkway with adjustable handrails on each side. There is some strength-training equipment in a corner and piles of crutches and canes. Hanging from the ceiling are pennants from universities all over the country gratefully autographed and sent by former patients. The number indicates how many young people are injured in one sport or another.

The gee-whiz tech equipment is in a basement gymnasium. I want to use it, but there is a tollbooth. My daily therapies include regular sessions in the standing frame, a device that squeezes me until I'm standing erect. My body has to get used to being vertical again. It has become lazy from sitting all day. Tolerating being vertical is my passport to the basement and work on the fancy robotic equipment that simulates walking. These machines require that I can stand for twenty minutes. The standing frame squeezes my body like a mammography device. I'm fitted into a seat, and a flat board presses against my chest and knees. As it is cranked tighter and tighter it forces my body into a standing position by degrees. My blood pressure drops. My heart is unused to the work of pumping my blood up to my brain, which is a vertical lift higher than pumping it up to my brain when I am seated. I become sweaty and dizzy. Twenty minutes is the goal, because rigging me up for the work on the robotic walking machines is complex and time-consuming. I am getting close, but I still call uncle before my required time.

OUR BOYS HOLD some magic power. When Matt visits he tells me to move my left hand, the one I consider as useful as a paperweight. I do. Hadrian's family comes for a visit. Matt likes to adopt a coach persona, but Hadrian prefers a player role: "You got to keep up, Jimbo." One evening he comes over to me and says, "What have you got in your legs?" I tell him not much. He takes hold of my right foot and pushes it back with a sharp jolt. My quads fire and my foot shoots forward. Then he grabs hold of my left foot and repeats the push. My left foot fires back. We all get a little hysterical. I push my feet back and forth and wiggle my toes! I go to bed with dreams of walking back into my house. The next morning Hadrian is there for a repeat training gig, but there's not so much juice and the legs don't respond. Yet while stretching I can feel my legs push against his hands. Some movement is there, not as wildly exciting as the night before.

The know-it-alls, Meghan and Caitlin, had warned me that my time here would be a roller coaster. How the nerves in the spinal cord talk to the body is mysterious. It isn't like training a weak muscle by working the hell out of it to make it stronger. Fatigue will make the muscle weaken and fade. The catch-22 is that if your muscles have no strength when the spine sings, it's hard for your body to dance. So the therapies move my muscles to keep some activity level while hoping that lightning will strike.

I tell Meghan about my foot-pushing routine with Hadrian and the disappointment in the morning. False signs happen, she explains. She suggests that we take it as a spark. We'll see if we can fan the flame. Something *is* happening. Meghan transfers me to a mat, where I lie on my back with bent knees, my feet on the mat. She wants me to see if I can lift my butt up off the mat. It's a "show me the money" moment. She counts to three, and lift off! Not exactly the moon, but there is empty space between my butt and the mat. The push in my legs is not just a will-o'-the-wisp.

Consider the wonder of your hands. We are all sensitive to touch and how we use hands and fingers to manipulate, give and receive pleasure, and do work. In my *You're Well and Truly Screwed Manual of Spinal Cord Injury* there's a section on "You Can't Feel Shit: Maybe Hot and Cold, but Don't Count On It." Hands will feel various ways: as if they've just woken up from going to sleep, tingling as blood flows back; on the verge of frostbite because they're freaky cold; or thick or fat, as if you'd been hanging upside down, a hunter's trophy ready to bleed out. The way your hands feel to you is not how they will feel to someone touching them. To others they'll feel normal. Do not think about all you used to do with your hands. There are jokes about this. You've done most of it: too bad! Thanks for the memories. Hands are part of personality. You talked with them; you said what you couldn't say in words. They gave you the feeling of sandpaper, a dog's nose, an ice cube, and a breast. They knew the difference between gooey and hard, erotic and affectionate. Once your mind was conductor of the orchestra of sensations, speaker of the language of touch. Now the orchestra is full of empty chairs and appears like an old, scratchy, black-and-white film with a bad soundtrack. The model and picture listed in the hands section of the operating manual is stamped with a warning: Original Equipment. No Reorder in Case of Careless or Random Damage. (See fine print under Fate, Karmic Debt, Crap Out of Luck.)

Caitlin says she will meet me in my room to practice daily routines. She wants to teach me to use my hands to turn on the faucet in my bathroom sink, wash my ugly mug, and brush my not-so-pearly teeth. I manage to turn the faucet on, rub soap onto a wet washcloth (not very well), and then smash the cloth into my face, dropping it several times in my lap as my grip fades. Next I try to brush my teeth. Caitlin makes the handle of the toothbrush fat with a piece of rubber tubing so I can hold it even with my weak-sister grip. I manage to screw the top off the toothpaste: forget the little brush, I jab the tube into my mouth and squirt in some toothpaste, then dive bomb my teeth with my erratic right hand to "brush" the paste against the teeth. I brush a few teeth on both sides and claim victory. I'm like a little league kid who hits a weak foul ball and is told "Great job!"

Next, Caitlin focuses on my eating technique. I put a U-cuff around my right hand. It has a slot in the palm side to hold a bent fork or a spoon. Rubber bands circle the handle so the utensil won't slip out of the slot. I can eat what I can stab, or sticky things that stay stuck to my spoon. Gripping a glass or cup is not in the cards yet. Jennifer puts a lapboard across my chair arms and a bowl or plate on the board. My right hand dips down, stabs or scoops, cranks the fork or spoon to rise slowly just over my neck brace, to meet my mouth as my head bends forward. The neck brace stays for three months. Doctors treat that time period like some atomic interval that can't be changed. Unwelcome absolutes are part of how I negotiate time. Doctors' rules make the brace an uninvited, attention-hogging guest that is thwarting my efforts to conduct my daily life.

Partners in a long-term relationship navigate each other's different senses of time. Some like to arrive at the airport early; some shave it as close as possible. Jennifer and I possess the two parts of that difference. I always want to be early and she hates to wait. When Jennifer and I meet, I spot her fifteen minutes past the time we agreed on. She denies this, but someone in constant motion experiences all time as filled and doesn't recognize gaps called late. Now, without two autonomous actors, our old time difference will not work. We need to find a new civility with each other.

Most of what you do, you do the instant you decide to act. You don't ask anyone for an assist or make a simple chore into a two-person activity. Imagine you are in my place. I have a list of needs worthy of a toddler that require someone's help. Jennifer is caught in these needs, which upend her life like a natural disaster. When I can't do something, a feeling surges within me that I have to do it *right now.* This is particularly difficult when I talk to Jennifer. It's too easy to not stop and think with someone I know so well. I see patients hit the anger button, raising the volume on "I need it now!" I do it, too. Anxiety rushes through me like a panicked animal, and before I know it, I'm yelling, going from 0 to 60. Jennifer is like a beautiful pilot fish hovering over my large and damaged body, but unlike the relationship between the pilot fish and the shark, I receive all the benefit while she gets little in return. Love is powerful, but it can be weakened by a constant barrage of thoughtlessness.

Our new reality requires us to renegotiate the way we interact: tone of voice, saying "please" and "thank you" like you'd teach a child, being patient, waiting for help when Jennifer is busy, and trying not to interrupt her. This is our new comedy of manners. Every part of a relationship creates a dance of tone and inflection. Civility is not a superficial politeness. The word implies acts of consideration and graciousness that build the space for intimacy. Think about when you and your partner are both completely naked. The erotic and the sexual are negotiated not with throwaway acts of politeness, as in "Let me hold this door open for you," but with signs that you will respect and respond to each other's needs and fears. Will I be shamed? Will I be used? Will I be seen? We want to create the richest story together, and civility creates the conventions that make that story possible.

How can Jennifer and I be physical with each other, fill the everyday needs of hugging, touching, physically connecting, and resisting isolation while we live our different struggles? We practiced these behaviors before, as any couple does, but now have to reimagine them. I prized my independence. Now autonomy is no longer something I can easily express. Negotiating the physical world is done almost exclusively with the help of others. My therapists are determined to find and give back a piece of that independence. Jennifer's journey is different. She lived with me as a partner, lover, husband, and equal actor. Now these roles for me are unmoored. How does she avoid adding new names: burden, problem, and duty? So far we have our sense of humor and we keep ourselves from staring into the pit, otherwise we'd be a little mad. If we were, who'd be surprised?

Craig insists on conversations between patients and caregivers, and schedules sessions to promote this communication. It's already a problem to be called a caregiver rather than a wife or partner, and no one in these sessions feels ready to say, or knows how to say, what is happening to them emotionally. The truth is, we are all facing a crisis that takes all our energy to survive. Releasing the grip of what I've lost will have its day, but not now. An intimate relationship is sustained by the electric current of shared feeling, and by the willingness to be open and undefended. My body's oppressive presence can be like the bad date at the bar that spends all evening talking about himself: a closed system that the listener sits outside of, waiting to escape.

This isn't the first time I've withheld my emotional life from Jennifer. That story also casts Denver in a key part. Our rush together—out of our marriages—became a wild landscape that I couldn't stop thinking about. Love is magical, but it doesn't last by magic. Do I know what I'm doing, what I feel? The need when we came together was overwhelming, like a storm that rearranged my compass and moved away to reveal a new space. When I saw that new space I froze and panicked and wanted to run, fearing I was missing something. I needed to be alone. I was a male cliché. Call it what you will—a conflict I didn't understand was ready to break us apart when we'd only just begun bringing our three boys into a single body called a family. We were about to learn that such things don't happen without serial bouts of organ rejection. Events conspire to rattle the already rattled. After a scene of being picked on by Jennifer's two sons, Matt, then a little boy, sat on his bed in his pajamas and told me I'd ruined his life. You don't tear up one family and build another without pain, tears, fury, and forgiveness. Love doesn't mean we escape suffering just because we thrill when we fall into its grip. I had to act the fool and move out.

We'd lived together for nine months in a condominium Jennifer rented after her divorce. Then for a year and a half we lived together in a house she bought in the city, and in that time my heart became at war with itself over embracing my love for Jennifer. I didn't know what my feelings were and said I was going to move by myself to the house by the river, which was now empty. Jennifer wept so hard it frightened me. I retreated to some ridiculous, cruel, frozen place of a locked heart. I picked up this and packed that, all like a dead man. If I let myself feel anything I'd fall into a thousand pieces, not knowing what fit where. In the morning Jennifer was still. She emptied herself into readying the children for school. As I left for work, she retreated deep inside to protect herself. Propelled by will, she bundled Matt off to school, and kissed goodbye a little boy who loved her. The morning light stole her happiness like a pickpocket.

I moved back to the house I bought with my first wife, Susan. It was hollow and empty, like me. What am I doing here by myself? Why don't I know my feelings? I have a history of stuck emotions. In today's sexualized culture, my sexual coming-of-age seems quaint and stupid. There is the scene between Susan and me on our wedding night. Coached by my mother, I buy a gift to give for the occasion. I think it is cute—already a deadly notion. I get nightclothes that are yellow, with small flowers, a bodice and shorts with frilly edges ending mid-thigh. The trouble is that when she puts them on she looks like a character from *The Beverly Hillbillies*. If this is a test of whether we can laugh at ourselves, we fail. We are both embarrassed. The next surprise for her is that I have never had sexual intercourse until this night. There has been plenty of near-naked petting and rubbing, but never the full card trick. As to the geography of a vagina, I am clueless. How can it be? A graduate of top universities, who has researched the avant-garde twists and turns of German theater in the twenties, doesn't know the operating instructions for the object of every teenage boy's fantasy. Perhaps this is another test we fail: one of us needs to say either, "Teach me," or, "Let me show you." It's an example of being stuck and not owning my feelings about my most basic urges. Need is easy; intimacy is not. The connection I avoid that night is not found later with more experience but remains lost. On the verge of divorce I'm in a group therapy session. The leader asks me to pick up a spongy bat and have a smack about with a woman in the circle. Can I let my emotion out in a mock battle with a stand-in for the woman in my life? No. I stand frozen like a tree. I feel humiliated and don't go back.

So, my conflict had roots. It took me to rattle around that empty house, and risk losing the person who knew

how to ask and answer the questions of intimacy. The
heart is subversive.

During my separation from Jennifer I was like a man
with brain fever. While locked in an internal conflict I
couldn't seem to resolve, I became obsessed with learning to walk on stilts. I saw Peter Schumann dancing on
eight-foot stilts with a member of his troupe, the Bread
and Puppet Theater, and I was like a kid smitten. I nailed
two eight-foot two-by-fours together, improvised a foot-
pad and a system to tie it to my legs, found a long wooden
pole, and launched myself up and down the dirt driveway by my house next to the river. I got better at walking and making stilts. This out-of-the-blue enthusiasm
gave me cover to ask Jennifer if she would choreograph
a stilt dance for the two of us. We were still seeing each
other. We lived in separate houses and in a new uncertainty: is this it or isn't it? I was the one that crashed out
the front door. She never locked it after me. She agreed
to choreograph a dance, and we started rehearsing in the
dirt driveway at my house. I built two-foot stilts for all
the boys and taught them the trick of it. Soon they could
play stilt soccer on the wide lawn next to the house. We
performed our stilt dance at a fall dance concert at the
university. In the winter I proposed to her.

That makes it sound easier than it was. Before I proposed, I went through speed therapy. I met with a therapist every day, knowing I must cough up the stone stuck
in my heart or let it crush what Jennifer and I had begun.
The process released dreams; my dreams contained a
repeated image of a woman sitting in a rocking chair on
a porch, blocking the door into a house. She is turned so
I can't see her face. Dreams are about affect. I don't know
who is in the chair or why, but I feel that her presence
prevents me from moving through the door. The work

with the therapist pulled the image into focus. I didn't know, and then, like a slap, I did. It was my mother. Who else in my life holds such significance and removed herself without a word? Suicide did not wipe her slate clean: she wrote something on my heart I have to acknowledge.

The last time I visit my mother, she takes me aside and pleads with me to help her. I say, "What can I do?" She has a handkerchief balled up in one hand and looks down at her knees. She says evenly, "Ask your father to come with me to see a psychiatrist."

The basement of our New England house is finished in knotty pine and has pine furniture, a linoleum tile floor in black and green squares, and a bar at one end. Dad and I walked down the cellar stairs over to the bar and took out a Scotch bottle and two glasses. We stood across from each other. I explained what Mom wanted, how important it was, how I wanted him to go with her. He knew some conversation like this was coming. He was stiff and tense. His salt-and-pepper hair, cut short, was jacked up straight like his body language. His arms stretched out on either side as he leaned against the countertop, ready to push away what I say. He is all lawyer, all defense. Without saying so directly, he made it clear that he thought psychiatry was a sign of failure and shame. He feared it. His guilt about his part in the pain she felt hardened his resistance. I was there for part of the story, how he trashed the intangible equilibrium of their marriage with an affair. A period of lost bearings, too much drinking, and cruelty until the fever broke. A leggy secretary was fired and my parents had a superficial reconciliation. He wasn't willing to go talk with some stranger with a notepad in his lap to unpack that pain. The furies holding my mother hostage fed on his silence. I was usually able to get through to my dad, but this time I didn't.

I couldn't force him, and I failed to help my mother. I was a kid in my mid-twenties. I went back to graduate school across the country in sunny California. My brother called me on the morning she didn't wake up.

The ghost in the rocking chair demanded acknowledgment before I could pass by. Seeing my mother this way brought her back into my emotional life after I'd banned her out of guilt and hurt from what she'd done. Nothing was changed, but something was known. Something closed was opened. Jennifer could be seen as she was.

Oysters Shucked

Waves startle at the shock of color, fall. Currents pull counter to their swoon. Fingered stems jolt up from a pressure to be. They ripple like a field of grass woven by time as shed selves reefed asleep.

She feels sand rush between her toes, a pause as breath is caught. Her shadow stilts across the beach flickers above a bonfire drinking the wind. A swell slides up her thighs thrusts her forward.

He parades a line of boys carrying wood. They feed a fire reverent to its mystery. All turn like a beacon, see her, the tribe waggles. Trotting toward her his shadow kites up a cliff, splish splash big as a tree he captures her.

When first they touched their fall rent air once stable made ragged. Their need their surprise lodged in the ground, a barrier reef. The wind stills, a dog barks, children shriek, a kiss.

We craft our stories in complicated ways, but sometimes doing and creating something together rewrites our emotions by restoring a sense of grammar and words

we thought we'd lost. Soon after the stilt concert I asked
Jennifer to go to Denver. She didn't know how my speed
therapy had ended. We stayed at the Brown Palace, a
famous old downtown hotel. I brought a ring that be-
longed to my grandmother, my mother's mother. The
ring had a small blue sapphire in a gold setting. It rested
in a red leather box with a gold stamp on top. It had the
look of another era: solid, enduring. Before we went to
dinner I put the box in a sock and slid it under a pillow
on the bed. Later, she found the sock and the ring.

"Marry me." The words are clear, wholly owned.

"Yes," the word she's kept in her pocket, just because
she could.

I AM BACK in Denver. It is doubtful I can pick up a sock,
but we are here together. Yet I'm gone again, stolen in
plain sight. How can I be found? Meghan's tactic is to
creatively jump ahead of my ability, challenging my body
to catch up. Her improvisations always scare me at first.
You'd think the body would be hungry, like a toddler that
throws himself around trying to walk, to push ahead,
to grasp for more. But what makes the toddler tilt over
and crash? I don't believe it will happen if he isn't getting
pleasure from testing his body, wobbling to keep balance,
then hitting the deck. Where is that pleasure happening?
Is it in his mind, chasing the goal of balance? In his body,
feeling the sensation of toes gripping, hips swaying, arms
waving, face flushed with concentration? I use two words,
mind and *body*, to describe this action. For the toddler
there is no division. For the seventy-year-old with a body
that is crippled, a division is manifest. The repetitive,
determined pleasure of the toddler is not readily available. In its place is the opposite: fear. First, the movement of the body into a new position doesn't feel good.

Second, if the new position requires the body to balance while standing, the mind can be gripped with panic. Eyes fixed to the floor, the torso becomes rigid; this body is a million miles from the relaxed body that is prepared to walk without a conscious thought. Even physically normal people recognize the division between mind and body as they go to their regular workouts at the gym. There are surely those days when they have to overcome resistance to the whole routine: changing in and out of clothes, making effort, pushing for more. There is no united mind-body seamlessly working out, but a dialogue that can either motivate or undermine the planned workout. We all experience this division, when we are self-aware. The word *discipline* refers to how we shape the division. It can be difficult for an average person and thus is only magnified many times over for the injured.

One day, Meghan takes me to a mat table with that look that says we are going to try something new. She leaves me sitting on the mat to go rummage in a closet, and comes back with a funky-looking harness, its straps covered in sheepskin. She proposes putting the harness on me and trying an experiment. I will walk a few steps, held up by an overhead lift attached to this harness. Am I game? She isn't really asking. It's a way to keep me practicing "yes" to all such activities. The harness has two straps that go on either side of my pelvic package. Much attention is paid to avoid pinching. I've gained the ability to stand up from a sitting position with some effort, pushing off with my right hand against the mat. Once I'm up, the lift line holds me up. Meghan corrals an assistant and they position themselves at my feet. In her best encouraging voice, that still manages to be directive, she says, "Try to step, Jim. We're right here." The lift line slides in the track above as I move. Crab-like, I move a few steps, with an assist on each foot. I'm easily fatigued, and the effort plus the panicky gripping in my shoulders moves her to call time out. I can tell she got more than she expected out of me. She is showing my body what it already knows: the movements of walking. The screen in my mind that can organize walking is full of static and snow, a mix of anxiety, muscles not yet firing, overall weakness, and whacked-out balance. Still, opening further the window that slammed shut between mind and body becomes the focus of my remaining time at Craig. How wide can they pry the window open with exercises and devices that mimic walking?

Some prefer to focus on mind as a force fully integrated with the body. I am not selling any spiritual soap. My experience is that I'm inhabited by something separate, alive in its own dynamic, often out of my control. The world of my mind feels messed with, tossed around, and sometimes allowed the gift of quiet.

Before, my body conveyed me wherever I wanted to go. I thought "coffee," and I would be sucking down a latte. I might have been obsessing on my phone, but my feet were a GPS that never required my attention. Now my body, if it's going to move again, depends on my mind's purpose, its effort to call on the muscles to move, its will to try and change what seems unchangeable. For a quadriplegic to push against gravity and stasis the mind must overcome discomfort, doubt, and anxiety, and give up what little bit of pleasure is found in remaining quiet. Quiet may become a self-fulfilling prophecy as the mind abandons the body to immobility, and the little bit of pleasure is seized on and turned into too much eating, distraction, or oblivion.

More changes emerge. I begin using voice-recognition software to dictate. Jennifer is freed. I have minor outbursts of cursing. My right hand helps edit. If my hand doesn't cooperate, every cursor move is controlled by a verbal command, like a traveler trying Dutch, only worse. One day Caitlin looks at me as if she's noticed something. She says, "Lean over your knees." Can I? Yes! This trick means no need for a chair that cranks back to relieve pressure on my butt. My tilt model is traded in for a chair with a fixed back. The lean over my knees is equivalent to the feet-over-head to release my ischial tuberosity, the lowest of the three major bones that make up each half of the pelvis. It is covered by what you grab when you're fresh with your date: her round, firm bum. She either returns the favor or slaps your face. I lean over my knees and unweight my tush. I no longer fear sores from prolonged sitting. I add to my small victories by beating the clock in the standing frame, remaining vertical for twenty minutes. I get my ticket punched for the walking machine carnival.

I'm fitted into a contraption that's a cross between a climbing harness and a webbed corset. Three people work on adjusting the harness as I lie on a mat. I feel the corset cinched very tight. They test to be sure the straps that go between my legs don't pinch my nuts. I'm being prepared for a session on a large apparatus called a Lokomat—a computer-driven robotic walker. The harness in place, I drive my wheelchair up a short ramp beneath the machine's yardarm. The crew clips me to straps on the lift bar. They raise the bar so my feet dangle off the ground. If the straps are going to crush my nuts, it will happen now. They'd be pissed but polite; they'd have to start over refitting the harness. My first time on the machine involves a long process to adjust upper and lower leg pieces to the height and length of each section of my legs. A strap attaches to the front of each shoe to

lift my toes so my foot doesn't stub against the treadmill as it comes forward. Measurements are entered into
a computer. A hard exoskeleton is strapped to my legs
and thighs. If all the measurements are matched correctly to my frame, the machine can simulate my stride.
I hang suspended over a treadmill as they measure and
strap. In front and to the left is the computer screen.
They start with me still suspended to see if the program
can move my legs in the air. They make adjustments to
smooth the stride. Slowly they lower me to the treadmill,
lightly brushing my feet on the surface, then allowing
more weight. In the first session, actual walking practice
is short because of the time needed to set up. Later they
experiment with weight-bearing, and they turn on the
computer screen where an avatar represents me walking
in a landscape dotted with trees and animals. By twisting my torso, I'm to steer the avatar left or right to avoid
hitting them. I have more hits than misses. It is eerie to
be held suspended by this apparatus, with my legs moving in the air. It feels like a cartoon of walking. It is bit-
tersweet to feel the motion as a puppet of the machine.
Motion is a drug. We are unknowing addicts until we
can't have it.

BOTH OF OUR mental fire alarms clang. We should have
seen it coming sooner. The day we will be sent home to
manage my condition for the rest of our lives is nearly
here. We don't want to accept it, but the rehab team
doesn't see enough signs of new function developing to
justify keeping me here. This alters the light and dark of
our moods. Jennifer is never difficult to read when she's
upset. She goes into her I-don't-want-to-talk-about-it,
silent-running mode. The silence deflects all attempts at
contact. On top of this she learns she won't have a course

to teach in the dance program next year. Although retired, she keeps her hand in the program by teaching Pilates and dance education. She feels the walls will close in on her life if she's only looking after me, with no engagement outside. Whenever she goes into silent-running mode it is as if she has put herself out of reach. I can speak, but to no effect. She knows it drives me crazy, but this is and isn't about me. It takes me a day to get her to speak about what is bothering her. It is sunny and we go outside to sit in a garden area where, a few days before, I'd burst into tears because my trachea hole hadn't closed. With the device removed it should heal in a week. At three weeks, mine had not closed. If the hole is open, I can't use the pool, one of the great therapies, where I'd be embraced in warm water and made buoyant against gravity. I want more time to work on my legs, on everything.

Jennifer starts to cry. She finally talks about the teaching and her fears of handling my care. She looks around at this garden next to a large hospital building and remembers her own gardens, our two black Labs, and our house. Have the dogs forgotten her? Spring is coming. She wants to put her hands in her own good dirt. She knows she can't stay here out of fear of being alone with my care, without the backup of Craig. So many people still deal with me. Two people in the morning, therapists who work with me most of the day, two people to prepare me for bed, a roving team at night that shifts my body and holds it in place with foam wedges to prevent bedsores, and a nurse available at the push of a button. If she thinks about it she really hates all this: the hospital culture, with ruin on display; the air dry and cold like an arctic desert; nothing from her life reflected back in these surroundings; and the sense she's being watched and judged by the staff around me.

It's past time to find a new gear. If she has to learn catheters, medicines, dilling, and the rest of it, she can. She's had two babies, survived cervical cancer, and endured the competitive cruelty of professional dance. She can own this. She seizes the tasks Craig wants her to learn before they boot us out the door. She earns her stars with the nursing staff. Although it shouldn't need saying, the axiom that women are more is again proven.

It is the first official day of spring. Persephone is finding her way back from the underworld. We've been at Craig since January 11. Soon we'll be home and Jennifer will be energized by her gardens. I'm more like a plant than not. Too bad she can't just add water and place me in the sun to deal with me. When we married, the Rio Grande house came under her sway. It had two acres of grounds that were neglected and undeveloped. There were mature cottonwood trees, a small orchard, a pasture, Spanish-dagger cactus and a large cholla next to the house, hardscrabble dirt, and weeds. The pasture covers one acre, and the grounds around the house make up the second acre. We can flood-irrigate part of the property, but the rest has been watered only with handheld hoses. It's a farming area that used to be flooded by the Rio Grande. It's now fields of alfalfa or corn, made possible by the drainage ditches built by the Army Corps of Engineers. The fields around us are on the flyway for migratory birds. Fall brings Canada geese, sandhill cranes, ducks of many varieties, snow geese, eagles, a blue heron, and a big flock of crows tired of the city. When Jennifer sees bare ground she will find a way to put it to work: she can't be idle, so good soil can't be left just to sunbathe. Once home, Jennifer will have her gardens to welcome her. She is a creature who comes alive between sun and earth.

Tea

Spring awakes her garden's unrepentant mob.
Like drunks exposing themselves, soiling the carpet,
hollering like babies, hair tangled, faces smeared.
Her rake's sharp tongues quell the mob mid-rampage.
Flame snuffs resistance; vapor trails make ash graffiti.

She banishes debris skulking in hidden pockets of sloth.
The dead dislodged complain; a promise is extracted.
Pyres release thick smoke; exposed ground blushes.
Insects sneer at the cowed insurrection.
She walks the perimeter expects tribute from the rabble.

A child rushes up crying, a plaint of wrongs done.
She bends, stills the whirling spirit in an embrace.
A voice calls her name; the child's father holds out tea.
Hands touch, a file from memory's cabinet spills out.
It traces a lintel's dated lines of a son's passage.

A hot wind bursts open a portal, thick smoke lifts.
A toad comes forth, his massive stomach heaves
He glistens in the day's light, this voyager from below.
Greetings exchanged, the wind sighs.
She asks, "Tell us, traveler, what news?"

Together we transform the outside of our home, a
kind of physical romance with the dirt and ourselves.
This is our routine. On a weekend, we work ourselves to
exhaustion until sunset, then sit on the porch and drink
gin and tonics. We get up, drinks in hand, wander the
property, admire what we have done that day, and scheme
on what to do next. As the light fades, our two black Labs
think they have our attention and try to impress us with
a show of wrestling, growling, and baring of teeth. In the
last light we go in, feed the dogs, shower, and make love.

We've covered the bare ground that made Jennifer anxious. In my retirement, it was to be our pleasure to work outside, erasing, redrawing, and restoring the canvas we created. Here's an example, with others to come, where I'll be at the margin of an activity with such meaning, and set apart.

I DON'T WANT to give up Craig's know-how. I want to push for more function. I make efforts to walk in order to seduce Craig into keeping us a little longer. It is time to empty my pockets. I need to show new function in my legs. They can't justify an extension unless I provide evidence of change that my insurance deems worthy. Soon my rehab team will decide if I've produced enough moves to keep us past our March 28 sell-by date.

I can roll from side to side when Meghan asks me, and I can sit on the edge of a raised mat and hold myself erect. This is not new, but still a thank-you-God move when I do it. Meghan calls Caitlin over to show off my rolling and sitting. It doesn't go well. My next session with Caitlin doesn't go well either. Caitlin wants to see if I can put a shirt on by myself. The exercise is a disaster. I'm not even close to this maneuver. My anxiety covers me like a swarm of insects. I've told myself I'm on a roll; I rack up progress in session after session and am not prepared for failure. I remember talk of coming to a plateau after a run of change. I jump down a black hole. When I run into Dr. Skelza, I rattle off my frustrations and failures of the day. I have no composure or inhibitions left; I break into tears. Everyone rallies and assures me I won't lose the progress I've made. I am obsessed and irrational. Why not?

Rehab is a funhouse ride; get used to it. The same week of my panic, I stand from a sitting position when asked, and remain standing as a woman puts me in a harness for the elliptical apparatus. I love this woman. She is older, fit, skilled, and experienced. I relax around difficult tasks with her and want to do better. If she is across the room and something goes awry, she materializes before I can go into a full hyperventilating freakout. I hold my stand as she buckles me up. Cue surprised murmurs, swelling music. This much confidence won't do. The next morning I feel I am going to faint when I transfer from my bed to my power chair. My blood pressure can't handle the sudden shift from lying down to sitting. This is a random work stoppage with no chance to negotiate terms. The spinal cord is the conduit of a true complexity, even when we are only doing simple things, or when the dazzling skill of our bodies, outside of our incurious awareness, fools us into believing our motions are simple.

Craig is not paradise: the serpent here doesn't trade in the knowledge of good and evil. Here, the forbidden apple is to say, "Why bother? Why try harder? I'm comfortable. Why do I need more?" At home, doing more will be up to me; there won't be weekly schedules posted on my door. Of course there is Jennifer. I will quickly sour our relationship if I blow off any effort to gain more with an "I'll do it later." The just-do-it focus comes naturally to her, whereas I do think, "Why not later?" I will need the exuberance of children. Like children, I have tantrums. I'm not reasonable when I'm all soapy, sitting in a shower chair, having spasms that kick my legs out, sure that I'll drop on the floor. Jennifer, unbelieving, looks at me and points to the safety strap across my chest and calmly continues. OK, I see the damn strap. I still want a Lenny Bruce button. I want to rant and curse about how fucked up everything is.

News breaks my fever over my exit date. Meghan sees me after the rehab team decision meeting. Her high-beams flash on: "I get to mess with you for two more weeks." The new date is April 11.

WHAT WE THINK is freedom usually is not. We think freedom means, "I can do what I want." But we can't. We're tethered to our consciences. I'm tethered to the significant people in my life who love me and shape who I am. I'm tethered to civilizing ideas that stop me from lying, stealing, and using violence to serve my desire. We love the expression of the body in sport and dance because it's removed, in fact abstracted from, the anchor of interior life. We thrill at the vision of the body defying gravity, escaping the physical limits of the ordinary world. The dancer's leap and the gymnast's vault exist as objective acts, uncomplicated by, separated from, and free from the context of psychic and emotional history. We are lifted by these images that align with nature's power and grace, untouched by obligations, weakness, and the monthly bills. The body feels most free and most pleasure when it is in motion. We jump, speed, slide and glide, jig and spin, tumble, walk on our hands, skip and roll, bash and crash, and race against anything, just to do it. We are junkies of motion's release and expressive focus, unless it is to swing and gyre at the end of a tether as a bungee daredevil.

We actually live in a bound world, a world formed of our connection to others and the emotions they create. It starts when we are tied to our mother, floating in her womb. I'm caught by love, friendship, blood, culture, and language, and by the need for conversation, stories, the presence of nature, and the pleasure of my senses. I am a figure held upright by woven cords stretching out in all directions, held taut by many hands. I'm not so different from Gulliver among the Lilliputians, eyes open in the warmth of the sun, speaking, alive with the fullness of breath.

I fear I will be cut loose. This fear grows from a train of thought that says this accident is punishment. I will be discarded; every face will greet me with a dismissive pity. I'll be nothing more than an object to move, clean, feed, and store. Thinking this way breeds the feeling that what waits is some kind of hell. I obsess about how this exile could happen, picking at myself like a carrion bird to pull loose some meaning. My efforts to connect feel small, deluded. What can happen to me? Instead of building ties to the world, I cut them, angry at what's been done to me. I convince myself that I am a freak, a brain attached to wheels run by a battery. The self I was is lost in my spinal column, along with my spirit. Isolation is what the devil pimps.

We can find him at his work in Conor McPherson's play, *The Seafarer*. The devil comes in the shape of Mr. Lockhart to play a card game among a group of friends. Lockhart is there to play a hand of poker with a character named Sharky. The stakes for this hand will be Sharky's soul. Lockhart has to draw him into the game and win; then Sharky will be his. Sharky's friends are innocent of this wager as they play. During a moment in the game when they are alone, Lockhart describes hell to Sharky:

> What's hell? (*Gives a little laugh.*) Hell is . . . (*Stares gloomily.*) Well you know, Sharky, when you're walking around and round the city and the streetlights have all come on and it's cold. Or you're standing outside a shop where you were hanging around reading the magazines, pretending to buy one 'cause you've no money and no-

where to go and your feet are like blocks of ice in those stupid little slip-on shoes you bought for chauffeuring. And you see all the people who seem to live in another world all snuggled up together in the warmth of a tavern or a cozy little house, and you just walk and walk and walk and you're on your own and nobody knows who you are. And you don't know anyone and you're trying not to hassle people or beg, because you're trying not to drink, and you're hoping you *won't* meet anyone you know because of the blistering shame that rises up in your face and you have to turn away because you know you can't even deal with the thought that someone might love you, because of all the pain you always cause. Well that's a fraction of the self-loathing you feel in hell, except it's worse. Because there truly is no one to love you. Not even Him. (*Points to the sky.*) He lets you go. Even He's sick of you. You're locked in a space that's smaller than a coffin. Which is lying a thousand miles down just under the bed of a vast, icy, pitch black sea. You're buried alive in there. And it's so cold that you can't even feel your angry tears freezing in your eyelashes and your very bones ache with deep perpetual agony and you think, "I must be going to die . . . But you never die. You never even sleep because every few minutes you're gripped by a claustrophobic panic and you get so frightened you squirm uselessly against the stone walls and the heavy lid, and your heart beats so fast against your ribs you think, "I *must* be going to die . . ." But of course . . . you never will. Because of what you did.

He doesn't collect Sharky's soul that Christmas Eve. The bonds between the men at the game are intricate, full of insult, anger, jokes, fury, and deep affection. It is a near miss for Sharky. When cards are put down it appears the devil has the highest hand, until one of the men finds his glasses lost earlier in the day and sees that Sharky actually holds the winning hand. It is the circle of friends, chaotic in their relationships, simple in their endurance, that saves Sharkey—all it takes is one friend bumbling into lost glasses to snatch Sharky from oblivion.

Ties, unseen but real, hold us to those we love. There are so many paths to take in life; it is a cruel fact that to irreversibly cut the strands that hold a life to the world is one of the paths. One morning in 1968 as I sat on a sunny porch in Berkeley, with the bay in the distance sparkling a defiant blue (an invitation to stand up, go, and be), my phone rang. My brother's voice in Maine sounds beat-up, confused. He covers it with his lawyer's certainty as he tries to unwind what's happened. I have to come home. "Mom's . . . Dad called. He woke me up. He was weeping, wild. I couldn't understand. I heard him say, 'I can't wake her. You have to come. I'm afraid . . .' When I get there Dad's sitting at the top of the stairs, leaning against the banister. He's crying; he points to the door of my old room. You know Mom was sleeping there. Something about the TV. I go to the door and call, 'Mom, are you all right?' I can . . . see she's not all right. Dad says pills. He pushes me closer. I see a bottle. I touch her hand . . . It's cold . . . I start to pull the covers up." (His voice breaks. Neither of us speaks. I listen as he regains his breath.) "You need to come home. I can't talk. We're saying it's a heart attack . . . just come." He hung up. She was fifty-nine. I can't know what gave her the terrible certainty that night. It is New England: too much silence and not enough of the Irish need to fill the void with talk, bullshit, jokes, lies, cunning, fantasy, anger, and affection, making a strong brew of humanity.

I have my mother's example. Why not despair over my immobility and withdraw—see my life as a ruin, a burden upon those who love me? Something else happens. My mind is the only thing not wrecked by the fall; it gains significance as hearing does for the blind. My mind thrives on the electric current found in the connection to other people. Most other patients respond the same way, judging by their status in that lunchroom as jalopies at the repair shop being worked on by their therapist mechanics. The conversation is engaged and laughter a constant punctuation. When I start to write about what is happening to me, I feel less helpless; my condition is less overwhelming. If I can say it, the words give me access to my body. If I can't have my body to use, I can write about it. Written, mine is a story with more chapters, shared not lost.

I continue writing weekly about my experience as a quadriplegic and sending it to my family and friends. Word spreads about my reports, and requests to be added to the e-mail chain billow out with names from around the university and in the community. Matt creates a blog site that only the family can see and encourages me to let loose about how I feel. We call it the WTF version of Jim's week. For a while the WTF blog is useful, but then I decide I'll say the same thing to everyone. In a world where strangers put their finger up my ass every day, privacy seems quaint. I have a new attachment: a readership. This fact is like a Jolt drink, turning my attention out the window.

MEGHAN DETERMINES that my state is not stuck. She asks in her "not-really-asking-dude-just-giving-you-a-heads-up" voice if I want to try walking again with the crazy sheepskin harness attached to the lift track. When we did this before, over a week ago, I did maybe ten feet. The track would allow for fifty feet. Harnessed, we repeat the circus of three people, one on each foot and Meghan coaching. I'm not feeling sparky. I'm fighting spasms. Poor me. I stand up and get motoring and lurching along. It feels better to move. Even though it is a pathetic version, some memory cell fires: "Yes! Walking! I remember this." Before doubt has a chance to interfere, I go around three times. The body knows. It keeps its own book, even if the text is garbled and the mind is afraid.

Meghan takes me to the big gym. She has a surprise, something to step up the walking game. Craig has made a safe-line like a high-tech umbilical cord. During the weeks before I am scheduled to leave, they install a new walking device. It is a track attached to two sides of the gymnasium. The track is about seventy-five feet long from one end to the other, with a curved, L-shaped turn. A line hangs from the track and hooks to a vest that fits around my torso. The line can read data and allows the therapist to control if the patient walks carrying their full weight or partial weight. It also controls how far to let a patient fall before being caught. Its great advantage is allowing me to try walking without any assistive device, knowing I'll be caught if I fall. I am able to take it for a spin a few times before we leave Craig. The concept of a track, a rope, and a vest lodges in the minds of our boys, to be brought out when we are back home.

The push is on to be sure we know everything about managing my care. Jennifer does everything she can without hurting her back, which seized up one summer when she bent over her vegetable patch. I carried her to the car and off to the emergency room where, hours later, the MRI showed that her L4-L5 had shifted. After some muscle relaxant and rest she was back in action. But she has to be vigilant and keep her core strong. When Craig moved us across the bridge, Jennifer's move into my hospital room briefly becomes a nightmare. Her foldout daybed has lumpy springs, which are awful for her back. She is told there is no other bed that can be put in the room, so she buys a piece of memory foam that makes it just tolerable. There are several tense back-and-forths with the staff about why a better bed can't be found.

Because the nursing staff changes shifts, one team does not always know how much a couple does to take care of themselves. For some the default stance is to peer down their nose like Ms. Grundy, certain you didn't do all your homework. Jennifer discovers there are a lot of pissed-off wives on our floor, tired of the assumption they are not doing enough. This is part of the tension built into our floor's purpose: preparing us to leave the hospital and be safe on our own. The nursing staff has a lot to keep track of, but in the week we prepare to depart they get blowback from strong women and they start to change their tune. Education is going on all the time now, both in therapy sessions and in our time in our room. I have a regular double bed, more like home, instead of a hospital bed. We practice slide board transfers from my power chair to the bed and vice versa. We try to imagine what a day at home will be like. We run this movie over and over in our minds to find what we've forgotten, what we'll need, and what questions we haven't asked while we have all this experience at our fingertips.

Another sign we're about to leave is that I'm scheduled for a procedure to install a suprapubic catheter. I'm knocked out, and a doctor drills into my bladder through my abdomen wall and inserts a tube that will attach to a catch bag strapped to my leg. Not surprisingly, many quadriplegics make this choice, rather than have a catheter stuck in their penis. But there is a permanence to the procedure that is hard not to notice.

It is a beautiful day, a Sunday. We will leave this week. We have some tears, a little warm sun, a little exercising, and pep talks about me bucking the fuck up. I daydream about a character in a fairy tale who thinks his future relies on a talisman he discovered dangling from a gnarled tree, glinting in a shaft of sunlight. After years of good fortune, he can't find it. He fears he's lost it and thinks it may have slipped from his pocket after a fall. When he searches his pockets he realizes he doesn't have it any more. The dream breaks and I see the wheelchair beneath me. We'll sail away from this island of youth, help, disaster, dealers in the drug of hope, and wise heads. There's one thing lacking here. Their world is not my world. If I stay here, I fail to escape the sirens, unlike Homer's Odysseus, and lose my way home. I would miss the point of the journey. Whatever I am now must fit into a life, not a hospital. Our ship is afloat again. Sometimes I think I should be tied to the mast and allowed to dry up in the sun. My body spent decades carrying around my head to good effect; now my head has to find a way to return the favor. Jennifer kisses me, then pokes me hard. "You can do better than that." It is she who came, a thief in the light of day, and lifted a heart, so good fortune is not lost. My talisman is not a magic object, it is looking at me.

Act Two

nnnnnnnnnnnnnnnnnnnnnnnnnnnnnnnnnnnnn

Sorry, that's close enough. Give him room. He's been dropped on his head. Too bad. Too bad. Oh, I don't know. Let's see. Can he stand up? Will he put one foot in front of the other? Can he keep the girl? Is he worth the having? Will he dance to a tune, Betsy June? Is happiness in the soup? How will the jury decide? Will they use division or addition? It is not written in the stars. The picture is pretty and sometimes not, that shows a man receive his lot.

CHAPTER THREE

Sweet Chariot

LIFT HIM UP, stamp your feet, raise your hands, pants on fire, lift him up.

Matt drives up in a wheelchair-accessible rental van. The front passenger seat is missing, making a space for my chair. A ramp slides out when the rear-side door opens. I steer up the incline and into the empty space beside Matt. Four straps key into floor notches and hook to the four corners of the chair to lock it down. Matt, a true LA citizen, expert at buying and selling cars, navigates the world of specialty van rental with ease to find this one that accommodates my wheelchair. Jennifer flies home early to make the house ready. Jason is here to drive Jennifer's car back. He's brought along his son Tucker, a brainy middle-school string bean. The last time Tucker saw me was the night I was taken away in an ambulance. I sit on my new, racing-blue power wheelchair. It's been specially ordered and fitted for me. Thank God for medical insurance, because it cost as much as a small car. We head south on I-25 for Albuquerque. This is my first car trip not organized by Craig. None of us realized when we set out that I need a gait belt looped around the locked-down chair to tie me to it like a seat belt. On Craig trips I was secured with a gait belt, but

Matt and Jason never saw this routine, and I didn't think about it when we loaded. I am like a large, ripe melon, primed to smash against the dashboard should Matt have to suddenly apply the brakes at freeway speed.

I am a quadriplegic with glimmers. I have signs of activity in my legs and right arm, but still need the full suite of equipment: a lift to move me off the bed, my power chariot, a rolling shower chair, oxygen machine for the nighttime, and my suprapubic catheter and catch bag strapped to my leg. The equipment I'm not sitting on or strapped to has to arrive at our home before I get there. But it isn't the equipment that worries me, instead it's what I can't buy or have prescribed. What about happiness? Where will I find that in the midst of all this medical equipment?

In the fall, before my trip to Mexico, I proposed an idea to my friend, Elsa Menéndez: Would her theater company Tricklock read a few poems from my just-finished collection called *The Menu* at my retirement do in the spring? She is an unrepentant fan and pours gas on the candle flame of my proposal to make a three-alarm fire. She plans to direct a stand-alone production of my poetry. The idea is crazy, but great crazy: an evening of theater based on a book of poetry. The performance was scheduled for the spring, when I was to retire as a fully bipedal organism. It is now that spring, and I am in a van in a wheelchair, worrying about the topic of the poem that begins *The Menu*.

Sorbet

There is a time to bite down and to slowly dissolve.
Why do we get the two confused, tangled in our haste?
You think happiness is ready at hand, second nature,

something put on the bureau at night when you undress.
But in the morning light you forget you possessed it. You
look in the mirror searching for a certain gesture.

Happiness floats like a gas seeping from moist earth.
It shimmers in shallow depressions, evaporates in the sun.
We claim it like admen selling toothpaste, fizzy water.
It's emblazoned on venerable paper inked as a right.
We line up, a queue excites us, a promise for a turn.

A grand kiosk waits for us hiding in plain sight.
You doubt and trouble, curse the luck, then make it up.
This improvisation is hard. What to do where to look?
It may be close at hand in spaces you rush past.
Loiters like a wise guy who smokes, lifts his brim.

Move in, wiggle your hips, see what's dealt,
Shoot the gap, grasp a hand, race the clock.
You'll stop gasp for breath shirt torn, drenched.
You spin around searching, a line forms, you run.
Fierce pleasure stings, chance deals a new card.

We find no kiosk on the journey south. We enter the
driveway of the home I've not seen for three months.
I see two black Labs bouncing up and down. I wonder
what they will make of me rolling down the ramp in my
blue chair. It is a bewildering moment for them, but when
they hear my voice, they whimper, bark, squeak, and put
their front paws onto my lap. As they push their noses
into me they feel my hand clunk on their heads like a
wooden block, not the two-handed ear scratch they were
expecting. They back off, watch me, and try to do the
math. They can't get the old number that says "he's the
one, the cheese himself," but I'm good enough that their
tails wag. I move forward in my contraption. Their distance after the initial recognition isn't so different from

what I feel when I see the home that has marked so many changes in my life. It is a joy to be here and not in a hospital room. It is also profoundly sad. I am not the person who lived here anymore. What I am is still a mystery. Jennifer and I won't admit that I'll stay in this chair, but here I am. I am a person who needs to be dressed, washed, fed, and taken care of, like a child who is neither cute nor cuddly. How can I think about happiness? I am a new moon in the universe of our home, with a gravitational force that requires every atom to respond to its presence and manage its effect.

At the hospital, there was little to remind me of my life before. Our boys sent pictures: a hike snap, a picnic snap, the grand old ones with the grand young ones snap, the dog, girl fab cartwheel, family and vacation scenes goofy and not, snap, snap, snap, snap, snap. We put them on the wall in our room to keep the hearth fires from going cold. Thirty years ago, Jennifer and I brought our marriage makeover, sanctified in front of friends, a tall woman with a Bible, and the three boys, to this house. Everything I see, whether all around outside or wall-to-wall inside, points to that other guy, upright on two feet, who can squeeze your cheek (you pick which) and do a jig. The Declaration of Independence says we have the inalienable right to pursue happiness. It doesn't say we get to possess it at no cost. What that effort requires is as clear as pea soup. I want the happiness gig to be up for grabs, but how?

Coming home is first about logistics. Do we have all the equipment? Is the house modified enough to accommodate a wheelchair? Where can we find a home healthcare worker to get me up in the morning and free Jennifer to manage the house, yard, and dogs? How can we find a driver to release Jennifer from my schedule so she can have some sense of her own life, along with time for her errands and shopping? The bedroom has to accommodate a rolling power lift, a rolling shower chair, and an oxygen-generating machine. Our bed has risers under the mattress frame so the bed height matches the height of my wheelchair seat to facilitate transfers. The bathroom cabinets hold gear for the care of my catheter, with day bags, night bags, and various straps to hold a day bag on my leg, along with the materials necessary to keep all that clean. Metal ramps are installed at three doors leading into the house. An inside door has been removed from its hinges and stashed away to make room for my wheelchair to pass. We need to figure out the medical support and how to replace some of Craig's physical therapy expertise. I want a physiatrist (a doctor who specializes in physical medicine and rehabilitation), a urologist, and an acupuncturist. Later, we'll need to buy a modified van to handle a wheelchair, so we can return the rental van, a pricey temporary necessity.

The next morning I dodge gravity. Jason, Matt, and Tucker are there to mother-hen our adjustment to flying solo in our home. I sit on the edge of the bed as we prepare to move me to my power chair using a slide board. Jason puts his arms around my torso. As I lean forward over my feet to unweight my butt, we twist together, and together we slide my ass across the board into the chair. After three months in the hospital I weigh 175 pounds, a loss of ten off my former self. Even so, seated, I depress the edge of the bed about two inches—inches we didn't calculate for when we matched the level of the chair to the bed. The difference means the transfer from bed to chair is an uphill slide. Jason assists as I negotiate the transfer. I fail and drop like a stone, caught by Jason. A lot of yelling, hyperventilating, and reassurance follows.

Our boys are louting about in the kitchen preparing breakfast. I have so many memories of our times there together, cooking and drinking, scheming up adventures, and discussing things to blow up on the Fourth of July. I remember the testosterone cocktail of young men jostling and trash talking to express spiky affection. I'm not prepared for how I feel now: excluded. Jennifer looks both happy and frantic. She is in the house she loves with the dogs, sons, and the me/not me she loves, but now everything is up to her to sort out. For example, the shower chair didn't arrive before I did. She works all day on getting it delivered, calling Denver, UPS, and the distributor until finally at suppertime it arrives. The chair is in pieces, like a kid's Christmas present. The boys leap in, and make it ready for use the next morning. When I glance at Jennifer she has the look of "OK, *but*. The boys will be gone soon. Then where's my paddle for this creek?"

We're sure it is possible to create a schedule for my exercise therapies that fits into a rational day. At first, Jennifer feels like a juggler with dropsy, balls rolling away in all directions. There are so many doctors to visit, so many insurance questions, and so many duties around the house. Then there's me, more work than help. Our ability to think strategically is overwhelmed, our minds like a brood of drunk mice attacking a hunk of cheese all at once. We are ADD central. Slowly our fog clears and pieces of our new life shimmer like a mirage. Start with friends: I need someone for home care; a friend runs a home health-care business.

Any help will give Jennifer a piece of her mind back. Until I'm hoisted out of bed, washed, dressed, and stuck in my power unit, I'm just a helpless lump. The greatest difference in my quality of life is between how I feel lying in bed and when I'm sitting in my chair. Jennifer frets about how little I'm moving. She compensates by side coaching: move your arm, work with your hand squeezers, do your exercises with your putty—all this while she's in full gear taking care of the house. Imagine how happy this makes me.

A writer friend, Len Jenkin, and his wife Ramona come to town. My department is producing his play *Port Twilight*. They stay with us, catching us in mid-adaptation. We are not a pretty sight. Ramona, a doctor, takes one look and rolls up her sleeves. They are dear friends and we have no reason to pretend around them. They see the hard parts of the day when we're both fatigued and I've lost track of my think-about-it button. I'm beside the bed in my chair. I strain to get into position for the slide board transfer onto the bed. I scoot toward the front of the chair, ready to lean over my feet and unweight my rear so Jennifer can twist and guide my slide across the board onto the bed. What follows is like an episode from *The Honeymooners*, with me as Ralph Kramden and Jennifer as the patient, suffering Alice. I bluster and panic that things are not right, that we won't make the slide to the bed. Jennifer is the perfect Alice. She looks at me as I carry on about falling on the floor and says, "Well, the floor is not very far. We won't leave you there."

Yes, I'm making a scene.

WE ARRIVED HOME a day past two weeks ago. One small triumph is that the bedside scene has become quiet and smooth, with a minimum of bleating from me. We have started outpatient rehab at a facility. I've been on campus and broken the ice about seeing students and colleagues. Jennifer, the get-on-with-it girl, announces that I should stand up twice a day. So I position my chair next to the kitchen counter and, like a supplicant at a tent meeting, rise from my chair and stand erect, holding onto the countertop. Yes, praise the almighty spirit we cannot see. Pray for this sinner.

What is this new thing I've become? I'm a different self. But how do I grieve the loss of the person I see everywhere around me? This sounds like drama queen time, but I assure you it's not. I feel a current pushing against me as I move around the house. It must be the good memories. There are a lot of them: they make a feature-length movie. But I'm not who I was. I'm a trailer for a coming attraction. Everywhere I look I see the past; I need to create the future. A line from a children's melody pops into my head: "Morning bells are ringing." How sweet. I need something more like The Doors. Or not. The band's name comes from a line in William Blake's "The Marriage of Heaven and Hell": "If the doors of perception were cleansed everything would appear to man as it is, Infinite." The infinite is too much for me; maybe that was lost in my fall. The finite is all I can handle.

In these first weeks there's no crying, but moments of panic, annoying spasms, a bit of yelling, dashing to this and that, writing my weekly report for my readers, struggling to stay awake (bagged by the sandman who lurks in my medicine), assembling doctors, watching everything change and not knowing what to make of it, getting help from dear friends, and trying to think about what it will be like to teach in the fall—to work. A fantasy I'd had of riding my power chair on the ditch road along the bosque is a washout. The road is so bumpy I feel like I'm a can of paint attached to a power mixer. In all this, I'm not finding a way to grieve the loss of the person I used to be. I stand every day at the kitchen counter, panicky like Ichabod Crane hearing the hooves of the Headless Horse-

man. I'm amazed at how Jennifer can play calm and collected to my hysterical and bug-eyed. I wonder if this can
all add up to something coherent, something more.

What's in plain sight for now: mangled nerves and
things taken away. Things like the joy of moving my
body, sex, feeling through my fingers, and the sensations
of skin. What's the matter with this sod? Why isn't he
throwing plates against the wall? Does he ever think of
driving his stupid wheelchair off the bank into the water
in the deep ditch next to his house? The answer to that
is yes. What is he holding onto that is so wonderful?
Does he think this story is about triumph? Do we expect
people who tell stories about their injury or recovery to
make us feel better? Surely we want to know life is valuable. We take it for granted until we can't. So is it up to
me to say yes, despite everything—the pain, the limita-
tion, the subtraction of most of what was once sensual
pleasure, the loss of freedom, of physical agency—yes,
the world still is seductive, still is a thrill?

Revenge? A fancy lawyer could be hired to sue the
bastard, pin the donkey's tail on some human actor, as
if the cosmos could give a damn about our legal team.
Oh, we're Americans all right, we try. An accident must
mean somebody is to blame; there must be some pocket
to pick for the negligence of the unlit porch. A failure
can't be inexplicable but must be turned into culpabil-
ity that equals cash. For a host of reasons—Mexican law,
the property owners' lack of means—we are not able to
scratch that vengeful itch.

I'm not bearing witness to the inspiration of courage or endurance. I hate what happened, but it is real,
immune to my interpretation and analysis, a new set of
facts. A tree that falls in the yard in a windstorm cannot be wished upright. Calling it beautiful will not make

it less broken. Yet something in me won't give up the world.

My sense of restraint is unreliable after my accident. My feelings include sadness and anger. Yet why spend the energy cursing and breaking the glassware, when that same energy can move my leg from its stuck position, despite how much the goddamned effort hurts? Anger is useful to say, "Fuck you, I will not lie down like a piece of garbage when I can see, I can feel, I can talk, I can think, I can love and be loved." Anger is useful when a spasm won't stop and I can shout the worst words I know. Nothing gets broken; just the silence. I feel better for it for a few seconds. Anger is valuable in therapy when I'm asked to do something ridiculous: the steam that comes with getting pissed about it forces me to make the effort.

I am at rehab. The PT has me sitting on the edge of a mat table. The muscles in my core pull my body left. No matter what the PT does to stretch or massage the muscles, this contraction seems to have no off switch. I have no way to stop the troll tightening the rubber band in my body. Is it a sign of better things to come, a kind of toll to be paid before I get more function? Or is it just a status quo for this injury and a sign of nothing? People tell me medical marijuana will help. I apply for it. A Puritan about my mind, I am wary despite the fact that marijuana is the difference between misery and a toehold on improving quality of life for people with many ailments and injuries, including mine. I try it in many forms but find no advantage. I earned my wariness as a teen, watching my father turn into a weekend drunk during a broken period in his life. He laid waste to social gatherings and his family as entertainment. As a result, I fear every mood-altering substance. I've found other ways to undo the emotions buttoned up inside. I chose art to undress my heart. Those devastated at the end of an evening can slam doors, make havoc, deceive, die, weep, then get up, bow, and take off their makeup.

One day we get a curveball with our morning coffee. My home-care helper can't come, and the service has no backup. It's been a while since Jennifer has done the routine of getting me out of bed. Everything goes smoothly until she discovers that the sling lift that takes me off the bed and puts me in the shower chair won't turn on. Jennifer has technophobia. Reading the booklet doesn't help. Don't take her blood pressure at this moment. There is no way for me to get in the shower chair using other techniques—they all require too much lifting. Skip the shower; no big deal. But I use the shower chair—a blocky wheelchair that has a hard plastic seat with a hole like a toilet seat—for the bowel program. Skipping the bowel program is not a good idea. If you're squeamish, look away. The only option is old school. On your side, soldier, do it in the bed. The romance of my injury never stops. You can look now, I'm dressed. Our gardener, hired in my former life and needed now more than ever, shows up at just the right time to help me get into the power chair. Jennifer says, "That was almost a circus!" I say, "That's why they have sawdust in the center ring."

We-won't-let-you is a tool for good and bad, for reformer and oppressor alike. Something is preying on my mind because I am having trouble with spasms and feel down and sorry for myself. Jennifer asks, "Don't you want to get out of that chair and get better?" And like the child I've become, I blurt out, "Maybe I don't!" Then I go into my litany of all the things I hate, and cry to finish the performance. We are preparing for bed. We are both tired and ready to burst into flame. My outburst is taboo in the catechism of recovery. I don't mean it, but I had to say it. I'd be lying if I pretended that I didn't have this feeling. I whine about how much this or that hurts. Then we trade examples of how much our bodies tighten and hurt as we get older. It was a real, biblical Job-fest. I can't avoid or deny the fact that unless I move, and move a lot, nothing much will get better. That doesn't mean I have to like it and act like a pious crusader. What helps is saying what I'm not supposed to say, admitting what I'm not supposed to feel. Speaking the truth is always more than the sum of its parts. It gives me new impetus.

One of the associate deans who grabbed the oars when I fell overboard calls. Will I pinch-hit as guest speaker at spring commencement? The invitee has a case of the can't-do-it flu. I will, and am glad to be asked. Here's my chance to cast doubt on the idea that we are cooked early and then are the bitch of fortune. I have fresh evidence from my fall.

On a cloudy May day in the spring of 2012, I roll my chair forward to the microphone and speak to the graduates before me.

> You artists and scholars of art already know a lot about desire. Yes, desire, the equal opportunity actor that knocks you down or pulls you up. It is the blind date you take to the this-is-my-life prom. The theme of this dance is, what am I: complete or incomplete? The dictionary defines incomplete as: "adjective, lacking, as in lacking a part that should be present or available, and unfinished, as in not yet finished or fully developed." I will dispense with the "unfinished" definition. Most of us think we are unfinished. We have a special drawer where we keep our kit bag of untried schemes. We open it, look, think for a minute about taking one out, and

push it shut. We know things are not really finished until the elegant gentleman with a hat black as night and boots cold as ice walks through our door.

I prefer to think incomplete means "lacking." Lacking includes the sense that something is missing. We all have some experience of holding an empty hand in a moment of dire need. Think of those imagined skills, that charm act made of vapor invented for a job interview that won you the spot. Then you have to produce. Or the date who hears your massaged tales of gritty fiber when you faced the legions of daunt to impress a fluttering heart. Payday comes. One of the legions comes to your door and you have to deliver the goods as she or he observes. Others won't put themselves in play, holding to feelings of, "I just can't, I don't want to take the risk." That passes for wisdom until you collide with a force that turns you inside out so what was closed in your heart opens. Some connection fits you like a key: it may look great in a bathing suit or come unbidden in any form, and seize you like a dog grabs a bone.

Every change in my life, whether career or personal, started with an awareness that grew from the inside that I was incomplete. It didn't come because I was such a great planner. It came with no warning and took up residence, a partner with desire to undermine resistance. Change is not always pretty. Desire claims to be an easy date, taking up with whatever helps get its way: guilt, excitement, pleasure, pride, stupidity, fear, or independence. The throw-down begins when your "I'm-just-fine-the-way-I-am" attitude tries to stiff-arm desire strutting with a new stunner on its arm, or fogs the windshield with a litany of: "It's too hard, takes too long, costs too much, freaks me out, my friends like me the way I am, just leave me alone." Settling for a defense of "I'm-just-fine" is a sucker's game. We may be fine. We can always be finer.

Yes, you've won a big battle by earning your degree. One day in the future it will happen, you'll feel something is missing and you'll try to solve the mystery of what it is. How do you solve it? Reality can often be just a matter of perception. Do you think reality is found in that device in your hand you check as frequently as an itch you can't stop? Some say reality is a thin crust floating on the sea of our unconscious, which occupies some ninety percent of our waking life.

Are the devices in your hands that chatter, show pictures, start trouble, and tell secrets proof that you believe the random things found in the book of your face more true than what people actually say to you in person? Is it because what others say in person is too organized, rational, and coherent? We turn philosophical when we want to be closer to people we care about. We can still be held by wonder: "Who are you? Who am I? What's missing in my life? Does it have meaning?" When we try to answer these questions, we reach for a language we don't teach in school but want you to learn: the language of intimacy. You'll ask these questions all your life; be prepared to be surprised.

I believe there is an evolution that is personal. It is just as powerful as nature's and leaves in its wake failed species that can't adapt. It spans our lifetime, and its mechanism is the discontent of being incomplete. You'll decide what being complete means, and don't be surprised when the story unravels and becomes again incomplete, overturning what was certain before.

You may go with the great tradition: the milestones of marriage, children, job, kicking butt, getting bigger job, age. Or you may become possessed and disappear into thought and practice, become unbound from the usual pathways as you build a discipline of doing that sets its own compass. Perhaps you'll do none of these things, but whatever choices you make will leave a wake, a debris field of folly and courage. Happiness will demand its place and a key to the front door, no matter what path is taken. As you cross boundary after boundary the passport will be stamped "Admit as Incomplete." on each leg of your journey.

I offer this poem for your travels.

Squash

Remember, you stuck all that hope in the ground,
good dirt, a few rocks, worms, and spit?
Then what, you got busy forgot about weeds?
You thought it would jump out, kiss you.
Recess is over check your marbles there's a quiz.

It's a day to thank the good dirt how the sun
Seduces the leaf to turn green make seeds
into babies, a slight of heart.

We feel the ancient garden, see the fat plenty.
Thank the serpent for spilling the beans.
Bring the harvest that holds the taste of mud,
rain, sweet grass, the finned waters ready for the table.

Make room, all are welcome. Fill your plate, claim the
day. When night comes whisper a story, eat a pie.

You planted hope now pull it up.
Break a sweat push against chance's fickle winds.
It's not so hard if many hands pull together.
Is it worth the trouble? You think it's free?
Show your teeth, feel the heat, taste the bit.

ABRUPTLY, we have an anniversary. Time churns along, not caught in our troubles. Twenty-nine years married, add five for the great, sorting-love entanglement. Our anniversary is unlike our twenty-eight other celebrations. Like it or not, it is part of the new memory book we're making. We live our day, we kiss, we wish for this kiss and another to lead to "let's get naked and roll around in the downtown." Instead we cast the dice of happiness. We see how different it all is. Don't make a head-turning fuss. Well, perhaps some fuss: she wants the me of "get up and shout and throw me about." But we go out, take in some culture, eat dinner, and enjoy friends.

We can't help but lay down a memory track; that's what experience does. Before my fall, I was listening to Proust on my iPod. He is one of those authors everyone says they've read or pretends they have. I had to see what the big deal was. When Proust writes about his childhood, the detail is like slow-motion images in a stereopticon. I swim in the exquisite detail of things and feelings he describes. He makes me think I was born without some essential ability to capture my own sensual experience. The past is never just the past. Proust's pointillist evocations of childhood reinforce my awareness of its shaping presence in my life.

Despite outbursts, I am more cool than hot with my emotions. New England tailored that suit. My childhood story sounds made up, a fairy tale for grandchildren. I walked a mile to school with my friend Walter along a country road, past a horse chestnut tree, to a yellow, one-room schoolhouse. It had four rows of desks marking four grades and a pot-bellied stove in the corner. A long table, built as a sandbox on legs, ran beneath windows that covered one side of the room. A young teacher, Miss

Prince, with whom I tipped over in love at first sight, held forth over the children of lawyers, doctors, farmers, laborers, and merchants. This school is where I socked a bully in the face from instinct that snapped like a rubber band. We were both so surprised that we became friends. Just up the road past the school was a country store. To walk to the store meant walking past a mythically huge black Newfoundland. He was oblivious to the reign of terror he created for the small boys hoping to escape his notice. Past the store was a one-hundred-year-old white church with steeple and green shutters. My brother and I came for Sunday school here at my mother's insistence, in her fond hope to tame her pagan sons with guilt and Protestant morality. She thought teaching us from a book that talks about the Father, the Son and the Holy Ghost would help.

My mother's emotions were deeply held but not easily seen. I couldn't help learning that trick growing up by her side. She was never harsh or mean; her restraint was full of care, worry, and love. I had moments when I surprised her and made her blush, biting her tongue to keep from laughing out loud. One day I rode with her into town in a big Detroit car, no seatbelts required. A little kid sitting next to his mother welled up with feeling and blurted out how happy he felt. I said I loved her. My mother reddened. I caught her off guard. I jumped out of the shadows, creating a who-is-this-kid moment. She looked at me like a prize melon that had appeared in her garden overnight. She, the daughter of Victorians, gazed at me all crinkled from a jolt of emotion, then back at the road.

Her dad was a heart doctor, never seen out of his three-piece suit, a wise and gentle man. She was the only baby of three that survived childhood diseases. Her mother was what used to be called a proper woman, her emotions held tight, but caring in her measured distance. My mother married an energetic country boy raised on a farm, bursting with ambition to rise up through the practice of law, taking seriously the fight to keep any tilt of the scales of justice fair. Their wedding picture shows a thin and elegant bride next to her groom's beanpole-happy-Adam's-apple-kinetic Yankee-Doodle force. My parents' marriage was a picture of postwar America: cocktail parties, cigarettes in every container, feral heat rising off the men and women who laugh, smoke, and dance with their dreams.

As my father became successful, they built a barn next to our house and became horse people. They championed the return of the Morgan horse. I think that, among the examples in my life of pursuing something you love and having the discipline to excel, my mother was a stealth star candidate. Stealth, because she was never one to tell of her achievements, ensuring that light was reflected on my father. It was that time. For several years, my brother and I tagged along to weekend horse shows where my parents competed in various feats of horsemanship. We were also part of weekend horse-picnic events, where a mother in the neighborhood scooped up all the kids and drove to a rendezvous spot where the horses would show up. We'd eat our egg-salad sandwiches to the sounds of clinking harness and creaking leather and the buzz of adults flushed with the energy of an electric summer day.

In the shows it was my mother who brought home the big ribbons. She had a beautiful Morgan horse called Rusty, whom she loved. She and Rusty had a special fit. Rusty was a chestnut with a white blaze on his face. In terms of self-possession, gentleness, and focus, he was the horse version of my mother's personality. It seemed incongruous to see this woman, who always looked like the well-spoken, well-dressed friend and mother on her daily rounds, become the take-no-prisoners horsewoman dressed in boots, jodhpurs, a close-fitting jacket over a white shirt and tie, melding with her beautiful horse, taking him through his paces in the ring. They became state champions together. I give this picture of my mother not out of nostalgia, but because she gave me my first encounter with the experience of terrible loss.

It was a summer morning. As I played in the yard, a truck and horse trailer drove in and backed up to the ramp at the front of the barn. Rusty was led out toward the trailer. My mother came out of the house at the same time. I don't remember her going to embrace the horse and saying goodbye. I remember her standing frozen at the edge of the driveway, clutching a handkerchief in one hand as Rusty was loaded into the trailer. No one said anything. The driver got in, started the truck, and quietly slipped toward the road. I remember Rusty turning his head to look at my mother as he was taken away. My mother wheeled about and fled into the house. I was just a kid about to go into junior high school, but even I could see that a tiny meteor had just passed through my mother's heart without a sound.

How do you cut the tie with such a creature, who is woven into your emotional life and has become part of your identity as a woman, with whom there is a bond of pleasure like no other?

Family life suddenly shifted to summers spent at a camp on a lake. Life went on. The whole horse world was folded up and put away. It was my father's plan, with no Greek chorus to explain it, no chance for a soliloquy to give my mother voice to unwind her grief. There was just the silence of New England, hard as the rock in its stone walls. I saw that silence leaves a hole that never gets filled. This partly explains why I refuse to adopt some closed, stoic attitude and retreat inside. I've seen silence act like poison. It may not kill root and branch, but it will take something you didn't know you really needed, something that gives life its elastic joy.

"CAN'T YOU JUST stand up?" Jennifer asks. She wants me to give up the sling lift used to transfer me to my shower chair. The seat is higher than my power chair, which makes the transfer harder, especially when I am naked. A botched landing on the chair that misses the open hole can mean mashing my precious, but currently useless, nuts into the seat rim. I've resisted the stand-and-pivot transfer from a lack of faith in the juice in my legs. I have a meltdown. It's my "gee-aren't-I-fun-to-be-around" behavior. Even I'm sick of hearing myself. So, I do it. I stand, pivot, and sit. No damage is done. We dump the sling lift; no more will I be hoisted and deposited like a sack of coffee. The routine changes. Jennifer or my helper puts a gait belt around my waist. She keeps a hand on the belt. I put my hand on her shoulder and, on the count of three, I stand. We are face-to-face. We might walk about the room together. Maybe soon?

Jennifer and I wrestle over finding the words to talk about my future. She thinks I should never yield to doubt about getting better, always speak as though I will reach the next goal, and never give an inch. She doesn't deny there is doubt, but even to state that I might not get better is painful, and she pushes it away. The brain is put on alert against the language of maybe and might; no conditionals are admitted. We clash over this because my natural bent is not to claim achievements I don't have. This is not about modesty, but because I need to state my doubts out loud. I typically will say, "Yes, it could be great" or "It could be not so great." For me, stating what is not yet true doesn't weaken my resolve to make it true. Jennifer is unwilling to hear the possibility I won't keep improving. To know Jennifer is to know how tough she is. This is not about tough. It's about heart. It's taken me a while to get it. This isn't a choice between realistic talk or happy talk. It's about where to put emotional energy and keep it undiluted. I need to speak in a way that respects this and doesn't hurt her. I can use positive statements when she asks how I am. I can make a stand for civility, instead of realism.

These conversations always take place in the kitchen. If the house were a ship, the kitchen would be the pilot house. Jennifer is usually cooking, preparing dishes for later in the week, making cookies because why not? She is the captain of nourishment, if not for me, then for the dogs. It gives her moral leverage in our arguments. I'm the lout on one side of the counter, having done zilch, and she's cooked two dishes, washed eight pans, folded the laundry, and hauled out the trash. She tries new dishes on me weekly. Unfortunately, in the love lottery, she got the guy with New England taste buds, not a great culinary adventurer. Something about being sent off as a child has made her kitchen the antidote to the snakebite of that exile. Her pantry is stocked for a siege. There will be no catching Jennifer unable to care for the people and creatures she loves.

People often say to me, "You're so courageous." I cringe when I hear that because I feel nothing close to that. What I know is that I freak out, I panic, I get testy, I yell, I want to be left alone, I want to be coddled, I want to be tough as nails, I want to be fearless, I resist new things because I get scared, I resist things because they cause pain, I resort to being a wuss, and I avoid exercises because I'm tired. I think when people use the word "courageous," they mean, "Thank God it's you and not me." It's not a mean thought; it's just a human thought. "Courageous" is a word reserved for something that scares us, that can kill us or lose us our job. What do I think? I think about luck. Getting better is a kind of luck. Yes, it means having attitude, a full battery charge, stand-up genes, support, and health as a practice. But, even with all of that, the fallen have to get up, messages have to flow brain to toe. The brain is a slut. It wants pleasure: sitting feels good, do that. It needs a dominatrix-will, character, courage—does it matter? The discipline is movement.

IT IS FATHER'S DAY. It joins our anniversary as a new page in the make-new-memories albums. It makes a kind of sense that on their day, mothers get flowers and brunch or a hike, and dads get power tools. Dad time is often conjoined to tasks a dad is doing. Fathering can be both blunt and restrained and make a harder dent. Fathers are often the principle of chaos in a family. That cuts two ways. When good, we don't have to eat on time if there's something more interesting to do. Risk, rules, manners, good sense: all can be negotiated for the sheer fun or excitement that might be imagined. Fathers offer a wormhole to an alternate universe where up might be down, noise is better than silence, and no one cares what the neighbors will say. At their best they are bits of antimatter to unnecessary harshness or cruelty from someone close. Standard-issue fathers often have an automatic adjustment for distance. They differ in the amount of judgment and encouragement that they come equipped with from the factory. Still, you don't easily trade in the one you've got. Sons and daughters have different math, but want the sum to equal love with ruckus, a hand when needed, and a full measure of belief.

FATHERS AND SONS always have a story. I left home to live the life of the bohemian. I despised the pinched judgments of small-town life; I disappeared in the exotic excess of the mythical Berkeley campus. Time passed and the "radical" became a college teacher, married with a kid. I brought Matt, already a toddler, home for a visit with his grandfather. My father loved fly-fishing and taught both his sons. On a beautiful early fall day, we headed to see Maurice, a Frenchman who ran a private trout-fishing pond and trout hatchery called Shy Beaver. He had a beautiful daughter I fell in unrequited love with as a teenager. Growing up, it was a favorite place to go for father-son fun and to keep up our casting skills. Dad took me to the pond with his new grandson as a nostalgic treat. We would help Matt catch a fish. We would fish from a rowboat in a wide, lush pond with patches of lily pads. On our way to the dock we saw a small pen with a young lamb that magnetized Matt's attention. Two fathers watched two toddlers, one two-legged and one four-legged. When a child holds a trusting creature close, hugs it ear-to-fur and listens to its blood sing, I imagine a question passes between them that will take its place in the child's life, enduring as the turn of the seasons: "Who will love without falter? Tell the story."

NOW I GET DRESSED sitting rather than lying down. One more notch on the "I'm-a-normal-person" scale. I sit on the edge of the bed while my home-care helper maneuvers socks, pants, and shoes onto my legs and feet, and then finally puts my shirt on. My pants are pulled up to my thighs. Then I stand up to pull them to my waist and pivot to sit in my chair. Standing up out of the shower chair is the trickiest maneuver. I have to bridge out of the seat with the hole in it. I'm wet and my butt has oozed down in the seat. My right arm helps leverage my butt and all things attached out of the hole onto the chair edge. The things attached scrape over the rim of the hole until my butt is in place. My feet can't touch the floor unless I sit on the edge of the chair. If they don't touch the floor, I can't stand. My ability to do this maneuver makes it plainer than ever that movement, rehab, PT, and OT all are contributing to steady incremental progress.

My insurance company chooses this exact moment to tell me I've used up the twenty rehab visits allotted for the year and that my request for more has been denied. The letter details the appeal process, blah, blah, blah. What to do?

At the same time the private sector fails, the public sector shines. How I get around from place to place for my rehab and whatever else I need is actually about politics and policy. A whole political party in our democracy acts as if government can't work. Those elected from that party do their best so it won't work. How can we afford to buy a van that will take my wheelchair? Vocational Rehabilitation is a federally funded program run by the states that helps people with disabilities return to work. Your government makes the difference between "stuck at home, useless" and "sprung loose, back in the saddle." In my case, they will pay the cost of modifying a van to accommodate a wheelchair so I can return to teach at the university. This is no small hand-up, as the modification costs as much or more than the van itself, which we have to purchase ourselves. Once my Vocational Rehab facilitator approves my purchase, they cover the costs of modifying the chassis and installing a ramp to make it ready for wheelchair use. We buy a used vehicle and, eight weeks later, we're done with the pricey rental and drive home in our own tricked-out ride. Help from your government to keep you a functioning citizen: Isn't that why you'd organize a society that collects taxes in the first place? But if you're the rugged individual who shoots and eats bear and wants no part of any damn government, then when the bear eats your foot off, you're alone with your Don't Tread On Me boast stitched into your tricornered hat.

It hit him on the head: Was he a match for what was constant resistance? Old Newton called it gravity. Now I have to take a bite to loosen its grip. How will I know when I'm at a turning point? I came home in April; by July I've burned through all my allowed rehab sessions for physical and occupational therapy. The insurance company's concept of rehab bears no resemblance to the reality of what I need. We take over the controls of my rehab. Jennifer is a certified Pilates teacher. I've taken her course in Mat Pilates and understand the work is arduous and subtle. She knows a therapeutic Pilates teacher named Colleen Cummins. I go to meet her. She is a tall, fit, pretty, keen-eyed woman with a gentle voice, rigorous technique, and an inquisitive mind. Before becoming certified in Pilates, she'd earned a degree in exercise science. Before that, she earned a master's degree in English and traveled the world, working in the high-end hotel business. She left that behind for a life in Albuquerque with her own business, two dogs, a cat, and a yen for adventure. Improvisation comes naturally to her, riffing on a deep knowledge of anatomy and musculature and an ability to connect to her patients: what they can do, how she can push, and when she can't. She is invested in, and fascinated by, how best to seduce the brain to partner with the body to overcome physical difficulties.

We begin working together three times a week. She's never dealt with a patient who has a spinal cord injury and has to learn how to maneuver me from my wheelchair onto the apparatus in her studio. The insurance world does not recognize the rehabilitative history and efficacy of Pilates work, so this is on our nickel. When Joseph Pilates invented the equipment and techniques of the therapy that bears his name, he first used them on injured soldiers. He befriended early modern dancers who adopted his methods, and now Pilates has spread widely, a favorite of the suburban and celebrity exercise cadres. When we start, Colleen does one session a week at our house, using our bed to maneuver me with more space than her equipment affords. In Jennifer's class I learned how difficult some of the Pilates moves are and how they call on muscles and core strength I didn't realize I lacked. And not just her average students found this true. Jennifer taught football players bulked up on weight-room reps who couldn't do the moves that their one-hundred-pound teacher, more than twice their age, demonstrated in front of them.

Colleen inspires complete trust. Like Meghan and Caitlin at Craig, Colleen becomes my pilot, navigating to find muscles she can coax to activate. She takes me as I come, uses whatever I can show her, and shows me I have more access to muscles than I think. Sometimes the simplest things are hardest to do, or at least they sound simple: breathe into my chest, don't pooch out my stomach when I breathe, breathe pulling my stomach up and in toward my spine so my ribs expand and my shoulders don't hike up. Within a few sessions, she and I try to move more parts of my anatomy than I knew I had. There is no atmosphere of Gut It Out or Pain Is Gain, no crazed fanaticism of physical fitness culture. I feel I am on a path that can lead to finding my body, even though that body is reluctant to be found and often sulks and refuses to play. There are days Colleen asks me for things I think are completely lunatic for a man in my condition. But she just calmly demonstrates what I am to do and acts as if it were the most natural thing for me to try. Craig Hospital and Jennifer beat my "I can't" response out of me. I work up a satisfying passive-aggressive grimace and pant as if I am in grave danger as I try her maneuvers.

The family plans to gather this Fourth of July. In the past it was because we're all fireworks mad. This year a drought makes that too risky. Instead, the boys have a scheme to build a walking track for me. We discuss and strategize about this idea over the phone. The plan is to install a sliding metal track, the kind warehouses use to move goods. It will span the width of our portal, about fifty feet long, attached to the ceiling. You know these tracks from crime movies. It's the scene where a detective enters a walk-in freezer and shoves a side of beef that hangs from such a track. It slides away to reveal a poor schmo dangling from a hook, stiff and frosty. The idea is to attach me to this overhead track with a rope that will catch me if I crash as I practice my steps holding onto a walker. I call Craig Hospital to ask where I can order the vest they use with their new, fancy, look-ma-no-hands walking track. I expect a big-city supplier, but the answer is a phone number in Maine, a good sign.

Am I ready to walk? Jason is an experienced climber and knows climbing hardware. He rigs the catch and release mechanism where the rope connects me to the

track. Pull up on one rope, and it locks. Unweight the
rope by pulling on a smaller rope to release the locking
cam, and I'm free to sit. I maneuver my chair below the
end of the track. They fit me into the vest, first seated
and then standing. Jason cannibalizes a shoulder-width
metal bar from the power lift I no longer need. The bar
clips to two rings, one at each shoulder of the vest. The
rope attaches to the center of the bar and to a sliding
roller in the track. I put my hands on the walker, stand,
and the rope is cinched and locked in place. If I lose my
balance or my legs buckle, the vest and rope will hold
me up. I start walking, one foot in front of the other.
One boy walks backward to steady the walker as I move.
I walked at the rehab facility, but not fully weighted.
There I used a rolling platform in a harness that took
about twenty percent off my bearing weight. Now I do
three trips across the portal and back before I run out of
gas. Each time is a little quicker. Everything works. The
boys all look at me and say, "Now you can do this every
day, Jimbo!"

Do we see ourselves? The boys have not observed me
for several weeks. I can't sense if I've changed. They offer
a tasty bite of encouragement. Although I can transfer
using stand and pivot, Jennifer and I have been using
the slide board to protect her back. If I stand and crash,
my size will mash her like a grape. Matt, fit from crazed
cross-training, is a perfect spotter. I do the stand with
him and try to settle my feet, but my right leg spasms and
I drop like a stone. Matt, strong as a caveman, catches
the flaming meteor and puts me on the bed. I explain
what I think went wrong. Jennifer interrupts to tell me
not to look down, to sit up straight and look at my boys as
I talk. I go crabby about her corrections. The boys laugh
and Matt imitates our bickering, replaying my whiny sob

story and Jennifer's bossy do-this chorus. Nothing like a little satiric elbow from kids to parents to show the ridiculous game we're playing, blowing a pup tent up into a chateau.

Stop in the name of love, but can she? A small circus materializes in our house over the Fourth of July week. There are twelve children: big, medium, and little grandkids with friends. Expeditions are organized daily to the pool, river, store, movies, or fishing hole. Meals appear, and table conversations cover politics, pop culture, and reminiscences. It is no secret that Jennifer's back is hurting her. Our house guests try to help her by taking over duties so she can rest. This is easier said than done. They have to be cops on the beat, telling her to cease and desist. "Ma'am, step away from the counter. Put down the dirty dishes." The boys know. They grew up with her. They play the card that I'm screwed if anything happens to her. She says how much it bothers her to hear that, because it puts such pressure on her. There's never been an easy way for Jennifer to relax.

You remember that famous biblical quotation: there is a time for reaping and a time for sowing. I think most people expect that, at some point in life, they will be dealing with their parents in the way they dealt with their babies. They will work with their parents' naked bodies. This injury has removed most levels of my modesty, but that doesn't mean our sons don't still feel it. My injury has confused the timing of the biblical aphorism. The boys shouldn't have to be messing with me naked. Craig staff was expert at hovering around and taking clothes on and off, and a cloth always magically appeared in the strategic spot. When the boys help me to bed, they too make sure the strategic cloth keeps its magic. We all feel the disjunction: I am a dad, interrupted. Something happened, something bad. And now we'll work to fix it. No, we *will* fix it.

The Fourth of July visit ends. At bedtime, Jennifer and I go through the stand-and-pivot drill. We're by ourselves for the first time since the families descended. We do the same transfer as when the boys spotted me. We realize that Jennifer can use my walker to protect her back. Instead of holding onto her when I stand, I hold the rails of the walker. I stand. We back the chair away because the walker leg is bumping into a small wheel on the front of my chair. I turn, trying to position my feet to sit on the bed. My legs buckle as if a string is cut. My butt smacks against my ankles because the walker keeps my feet from sliding forward. My messed-up left knee screams as my foot jams against my backside. I roll on my side to relieve the pain. My right shoulder hits the floor and my head ricochets off a bookcase beside our bed. Jennifer also falls. We look at each other lying on the floor and think, "How in hell did this happen?" We were doing so well. We are breathing hard, trying not to freak out. Our lift is stored and cannibalized for the walking track. We call neighbors, who come and right the picture we've skewed. The fall scares us and shakes our confidence. It is hard not to overthink it. We have someone spot us the next few nights. Again, there's the very same fall, butt to heels. I'm sitting with my knees in front of my face, the bad knee doing its fire alarm act. Luckily, we have guests who heave me back into my chair. We have a groove, mentally moving along a rising spiral. Any evidence that points downward is pushed away. But there's no denying we're spooked. The leg buckling feels like an ambush. We obsess about the fall, trying to keep it unbiblical.

"Lonely." This is Jennifer's answer to a question I ask

her. She means she is missing the ways we had physical contact before. Now when I come up and pat her butt, I'm like a Studebaker driving next to her, my arm coming out the window to give her a squeeze: affection in the traffic lane. At the moment, I offer one-armed affection. But "lonely" is a powerful word. It peels back a bit of the curtain drawn over our former life. There is an asymmetry between us as physical creatures. How can we be a couple again and not just a medical relationship? She looks at me and thinks, "There is my former lover, in a small powered vehicle. He is skinny. He can't stand up and pick me up. He is dependent on me. That freaks me out. He whines and panics. That's not so attractive. There he is with his ski jump nose. The jump is a little bigger than when I met him. I guess I'll give him a kiss anyway—better than not. But he has to escape from his brain to think about kissing me back or pinching my butt. He has to think about the subject of me. So, we will start with doing something we used to do. Sit on the east porch, watch the weather at the end of the day, and sip our gin-and-tonics. I'll have a real one, he'll have a not-real one, and the dogs will be in the grass, the fish in the pond, and the living will be queasy."

I DON'T KNOW what trick of the brain is causing me to shout "Fuck!" and bang my fists against anything handy. Jennifer dignifies my tantrum by calling it fighting spirit. Nothing yet works to stop the one specific spasm that pulls my trunk to the left. I'm told that muscle tone is essential, even when you're normal, so this increase in tone may be a sign something is changing for the better. But the sideways tug makes me feel like some demon spawn or alien microbes are about to burst out of my belly. Jump out of my skin is what I'd like to do, because being in this skin is an out-of-control carnival ride. The mysterious post office in my brain is busy again, but doing what? I don't know whether the letters are going to the wrong address, or too many letters are going to the same address, or simply no one knows how to read them when they arrive. It drives me bat-shit crazy. In the vest, on the track today, I make six circuits without stopping, just a swearing, raging, walking fool.

I think about my efforts when I'm alone, without any coach or therapist, a judgment born in idle moments. There won't be any Christmas calendar of my body in workout attire. There wouldn't have been, even if I hadn't fallen down. There's nothing to see but the burden, the cruel truth of age. However, the older brain sometimes is bigger, smarter, and happier. It is as if the brain absorbs the body's strength, fattening up its wise folds. Young is all hard muscle, hard knocks, and hard heads. Wisdom is not part of the equipment for running the hundred-yard dash or diving off the ten-meter platform and hitting the water at thirty miles an hour.

We have developed something like a therapy swarm for my body: I do repetitions on the walking track at my house each morning, Pilates therapy twice a week, physical therapy at a rehab facility twice a week (the insurance clock turned to a new year and reloaded rehab sessions), and acupuncture once a week. A quick inventory: I still need the power wheelchair, the suprapubic catheter with a capture bag attached to my leg, and a home health-care assistant to help me dress and shower. The power lift is in storage; I stand and pivot from bed to chair and back. I travel in a wheelchair-accessible van with a driver. I am just past the six-month mark since my accident, in the two-year window where greatest function may—no, will—return.

The question of why bother fades. My bases are covered. With my driver and wheelchair-accessible van, I can get around town and meet people, work in my office, and teach at the university. I have most of the elements of a life. I am three months home from Craig. Our state of mind is that somehow this is like a terrible flu. You can get over it, if you wait and work on it like a puzzle. In my situation, reason is not all it's cracked up to be. When they tell us "Return can happen," what we hear is "Return will happen." Staying alive is more than staying alive. Effort becomes an attitude. "Get fate's fat ass off me."

Perhaps I went past that "teach at the university" part too fast. In the fall semester, a year after Matt called to invite us to Mexico, I'm teaching one course in the dramatic writing program. It's a course in revision, helping the students graduating this spring shape the play that will be their thesis production for their MFA degree. I'm also advising the graduate students in the program. Going back to teaching should be another notch on my back-to-normal belt. It isn't. Preparing material and managing the work of the course is frustrating, because the simplest tasks of getting a book, moving files, and writing comments on work is maddeningly laborious. I don't feel opened up to a new way of teaching because of what's happened to me. I feel more like asking, "Why am I here?" If I were younger it might be different, but I retire at the end of the year. This chapter is really over. My wheelchair identity simply magnifies what feels like an unavoidable message: the department has moved on, and I'm a curiosity graciously given a final lap. It is still a pleasure to see students discover their voice in their work and help them navigate the byzantine bureaucracy of graduation. But an inordinate percentage of my mind and attention are taken up with my body in the fight to reclaim "normal." It creates a distance in my engagement in the classroom that doesn't feel right.

Two years is what everyone tells me. I hear it at the advanced rehab hospital and from the local doctor, and read it in the literature. Yes, two is sometimes modified to five to ten, but that's said as a vague reassurance. What I hear and see instead is a flashing billboard with loudspeakers: "You have two years!" A commandment, "Move," is branded onto my forehead. The two-year window is cosmic roulette. Do I have any control over what function will fly in the window? Is it luck of the draw, or are there extra points earned for effort? No matter, I carry that calculator in my head: two years minus the date. I'm on an elevator ride between euphoria and resignation, depending on how my body feels.

Have I hit a wall? Is this it? Do I take comfort, settle for what I have, just be? I push these questions away. Instead I try: What change will come out of the closet? Do I try for independence: get out of my face; I can do it? Is the choice between "make the effort" or "let go and nature will take its course?" The stakes are higher than putting my pants on by myself. At my age, this isn't a decision in immaculate isolation. I have a track record.

I have left the evidence of that record at the university where I worked for thirty-seven years. In that time I was the dean of the College of Fine Arts and chair and faculty member of the Theatre and Dance Department. My stint as chair caused a what-can-I-do-besides-go-brain-dead-in-meetings moment that led to creating a graduate program in dramatic writing and establishing an endowment to support it, even though at the time I knew next to nothing about fundraising. You think I'm going to sing, "I am the very model of a modern Major-General, I've information vegetable, animal, and mineral." Actually, I want to blow up two bromides that relate to this fix that has me firmly in its grip. These bromides, told to me more than once by accomplished people smarter than I, are: no one cares and no one changes. The first is used to steel an artist against any illusions that his or her individual marks on our physical world matter to anyone. Its truth doesn't matter; its cynicism does. Work that flows from a cynical heart is a cold dish usually left untouched when the guests leave. Caring is in the doing.

I came to my university career fresh-baked from the sixties. Things were serious in the world. Everywhere, people my age ditched the choices of our parents, abandoned what was commercial or profit-making, turning our backs on the pursuit of security. There are many ways to be a young professor. The usual calls for creating an expertise or a practice that becomes a shield that can survive scrutiny and be a knight's armor in the fight for tenure. That route leads to conservative choices about what to explore and is quick to shun experimentation for fear of exposing weakness or failure. Whether it was the influence of the sixties or my Maine naïveté and stubbornness, that path held no appeal. I chose situations that put me on the edge of what I knew, teaching subjects and creating work I'd not done before because it made me feel alive. I played a central part in instituting a radical reimagination of the department's undergraduate degree, pitting old against new in the faculty. My directing favored making original experimental work with the students, picking contemporary writers, and taking chances in staging that didn't always succeed. I was hard to define. I taught both studio and academic courses and enjoyed administrative work.

Too much zest can look like a pest. Not a modern Major General move, it got me into a lot of trouble. It nearly got me fired at tenure time. A friend, a white-coated doctor, took me to lunch during my tenure crisis. He was alarmed that someone my age, now in my early forties, could find himself in such a position, about to lose his job. He made it clear, if I had any doubt, that the world in general, and he in particular, thought risk-taking was horseshit. Grow up! But because of luck, dumb or rare, I didn't get fired. I didn't have to sacrifice my belief that risk is at the heart of learning. Risk is change. People can and do.

CHAPTER FOUR

Hot-Wired

WILL THE STORY reveal secrets? Will a human wreck snatch a measly victory from unforgiving soil? See the grit, the grasping; hear a grinding racket as something tears loose. Can the cow jump over the moon? Will the girl pack her bags? What's the answer? Do you roll it, smoke it, eat it, kiss it, make it talk, give it back, give it away, drink it, slap it, or share it?

The ability to stand and walk using various devices causes something to happen to my brain. Call it the *Chariots of Fire* effect. I cast myself in a drama of recovery because the curtain widens and I can see a little more color fill the scene when I make the effort. I hear the music swell and the waves crash on the beach. My gains reinforce an expectation that the virtue of effort will bring a reward. I don't think the doctors know why spinal cord return mostly happens in the two years after the injury. Nor do I think they even know why some people get more return than others. I decide to believe the music and am pushed along by a family that believes it will happen. What I am—the trouble that won't be named—is temporary. The natural state of being is to move. I can't expect my body to recover if it doesn't move. So I walk back and forth, back and forth. I am a cult follower in

Pilates. I do whatever Colleen asks, even when I say to myself that it's not remotely in the realm of possibility. Her voice holds steady encouragement as well as determination. How can I be a wuss in front of this woman? Moves I think are beyond the pale become doable.

There is nothing brave about my behavior in all this; I have to believe something will get better. I am an improvement project. I am a sucker for the belief that problems can be solved and things made better; that is the natural order if enough attention is paid. I am an acolyte of this belief: agency matters, fate can bugger off. Talk of how I'm screwed or on the downward slope makes me panic. Whatever the trouble, it has to be fixable, made better. I infuse my reading of the Greeks with the spirit of Walt Whitman. The Greeks know you are screwed. They teach: look it in the face; you will not collapse or cower at catastrophe. Easier said than done.

My acupuncturist, Jason Hao, is a specialist in cranial acupuncture. He wrote a book on the method. When he works on me, he takes my pulse in each wrist and asks me to stick out my tongue. He writes notes on what's going on with my body. He wears a doctor's white coat and carries needles in his left coat pocket. After hearing about specific issues with my leg spasms or bladder, he takes a cotton ball and swabs six to seven points on my head and a couple of points on my left ear with alcohol. He reads my head as a map of my body and its organs. Next, he takes out a needle and sticks it in one of the points and wiggles it. All needles in, he gives them all a good wiggle and leaves me for about fifteen minutes. He returns and tells me a story about a twelve-year-old girl from Dallas who came to him because she had a stroke in the womb that caused one of her hands to stay closed in a fist. Her parents tried everything, but nothing worked. Her left side also was affected, causing her to walk with an abnormal gait. At the beginning of the first session, he asked her what she wanted. She wanted to open her closed hand and shake his. At the end of her first session, he tells me, that's just what she did. After three more sessions she could walk almost normally. Jason was born and trained in China. He has written textbooks and goes back regularly to teach. He bristles with confidence and takes genuine delight in his ability to help heal young people. He often has a story of some success with unlocking a frozen limb or restoring a child's ability to speak or walk. His stories make me wish for the elastic brain of a child. At each visit he listens to my tales of my body and then needles me accordingly. I want the miracle he makes happen with kids. He's treated spinal cord injuries before. He thinks my case will take longer, but believes there is reason to hope. How could he say there is not?

What does progress feel like? At a rehab facility I do laps back and forth in a long corridor using a rolling apparatus called a LiteGait. I am held and attached by a vest. It can adjust the amount of weight I bear when I walk. A PT walks alongside me, telling me about research that says repetition is important to bring return with spinal cord patients. This is not what I want to hear. Repetition is a milk train, not an express. The PT says repetition regrooves the nerve track over and over, thickening the nerve bundle that makes the specific function work. I want everything to hurry up. I am in the land of the turtle and want to be the rabbit.

Progress is accompanied by the constant feeling that my legs have gone to sleep; they tingle and want to buckle as I step on them. I have shaky balance, so I cling to the LiteGait too hard from a fear I'll fall. The contraction in my left side still pulls so that I can't straighten

up. My left leg is weaker and drags. I pull my trunk to
go right against the leftward force, but I'm not strong
enough to counter it. To get a rhythm, I have to beat
back this wind blowing me to the left. Even in the midst
of this bullshit, progress happens. Usually I do two trips
up and down the hall at rehab, sixty feet one way, and
then I have to sit down. Today I do four trips, with no
sitting down in between. On my walking track at home
I used to do two circuits across the porch and back, then
sit down to rest. A circuit is about forty feet. I walk five
circuits without stopping and then another five after a
rest. I can open and close my hands and touch the ends of
my fingers to my thumb. Stand and pivot is more secure.
Lying prone in bed, I can maneuver my right leg over the
edge, then push up with my right elbow and arm to lever
myself into sitting position. If progress were measured
in green stamps for tradable goods, I'd have more than
enough for small kitchen appliances and be heading toward living room furniture.

I want my wheelchair to go the way of the dodo. At
rehab I work on the transition from sitting in a chair to
standing. The PT stands in front of me and positions
his knees against mine. I put my hands on his shoulders and lean forward over my feet. He pushes his knees
against mine, helping to lever me to a standing position.
We work on eliminating the knee trick so I can stand
without the assist. First we try having me sit at the end
of a parallel bar unit so I can pull up with my hands on
the bars. Next I try the maneuver with a walker in front:
my left hand is on the walker, my right hand pushes off
the arm of my chair, and I stand. I practice moving,
kept safe by traveling back and forth between the parallel bars. I move to open space with the walker as the
PT hovers. The walker is a standard-issue metal walker

with sides that fold. It's a thrill to be upright under my own steam, free of the power wheelchair and the umbilical-cord tether of the LiteGate and my walking track. "Stand on your own two feet" is what we are told growing up—no excuses, be your own person. To look at the world from a seated position and to look at it standing up is a difference of kind, not degree. To stand next to Jennifer with my walker, rather than look up at her from the wheelchair, makes me feel less the invalid and more like the dog with stitches he's not supposed to lick, crashing around with a plastic cone on his head. When I stand and stagger around I feel less like the butt of a cosmic joke than when I'm stuck seated like a Buddha.

Struggling to move, I confront my image in the mirror. I see an unstable body. Age is written all over it, from sagging muscle tone to lines in my face and wrinkly skin. The reflection brings up memories of my father. He is the closest family example I have of someone who fought a life-changing physical condition. I remember his thin legs and long, narrow feet stretched out on a couch in his knotty-pine-paneled den. It was the seventies. I was learning the ropes in my first teaching job. I'd come to visit after an SOS about his health and state of mind. He was covered with a knit afghan; his long fingers laced together on his chest. The afghan had been in that room since I was a child. It was familiar from times my father ate bread and milk on Sunday evenings, the knitted squares over his knees as we all watched *The Ed Sullivan Show*. He was miserable: hair matted, moaning, eyes fixed somewhere off in the distance, disengaged, and depressed. He and my stepmother wintered in Florida, where his troubles began. She was a short, buxom woman who hadn't signed on for the sickness part of "in sickness and in health." She'd signed up for the Frank-isa-catch part. They'd had a go at it. He married her. He forgot that what comes up can stay down. On an earlier visit, we'd had an awkward conversation as I was leaving. His erection isn't working for the sex part. I don't know what he thinks I can do. I am not exactly a dick expert. There were no little blue pills in those days. He is looking for relief: someone who has sympathy, who he feels is safe. I guess the hard-on gone AWOL took a blowtorch to the bloom of their early bed-a-thon romance. I can see he is distraught. Apparently my stepmother isn't forgiving.

My father had a history of the medical kind of heart trouble. In Florida he went to see a heart doctor, who arranged to give him a strenuous heart test. It was a flaming disaster. In this test, the doctor injected dye into the heart to see how the arteries functioned. The doctor, whether a predator on visiting snowbirds or just a careless hack, misjudged his elderly patient's ability to withstand the stress of the test. The doctor barely averted a fatal heart attack. He didn't test Dad's kidneys before injecting the dye. If he had, he'd have known they were failing. This discovery was the cause of his misery when I found him on the couch. He had been flown back to Maine and put on dialysis. When I came to visit he'd been on dialysis for a year. A year of scrubbing his blood gave him enough energy to have a social life. Then something changed. He barely spoke. He'd sunk beneath the surface of a depression. He had no more resistance to the assault on his body. And now my thirty-year-old self that watched his father suffer has reached the same age as the ailing man on the couch.

My stepmother was not a great nurse. How do I know? The same way you know your supersized uncle will have a second slice of pie. The threads of kindness between them were frayed. She performed the role of nurse because I was there. I am not a great nurse myself. I saw my mother latch onto illness as an emotional retreat and a cudgel in her relationship with my father. I am not good around sickness and am unable to perform the role of nurturing bedside buddy. I become conflicted and distant. Crap flows downstream. I see his face when I look in the mirror to shave, his same fine, white hair, his nose. When I lie on my back, I fold my hands on my chest the same way. When my body hurts, I grimace and make noises the way he did.

I felt out of place in the Maine winter light that held the room hostage from the window behind the couch. I wanted the golden light of California that releases explosions of energy: think it, do it. There in the hard-edged New England light of stone walls and few words, I watched my dad disappear. That night, he fell trying to reach the bathroom. My stepmother yelled, "Man overboard!" I found him on the floor, on his back, in need of a life preserver. He had to go to the bathroom but didn't make it; on the floor are small, hard pellets that fought their way out under the atmospheric pressure of loss. It was a fall in a fight he would soon lose. He moaned but brought no words to the surface.

This country lawyer could have made the dourest Mainer open his mouth and talk as if he were confessing to a priest. I'd seen him stop beside the road when he spied an original congregant. In flannel shirt, suspenders, and boots, the discovered backwoods sphinx traded precious words kept shut away from knaves and fools, for my father's bag of yarns and shoe-leather wisdom. The rustic philosopher and crafty trial lawyer was adrift in an agitated silence. I missed the man who wasn't there: the captain of his ship with a bag full of catch, commanding his galley. He has Scotch in one hand, a carving knife in the other, and an apron tied around his small pot-belly. With rolling pin, crackers, and melted butter before him, he is ready to prepare his special version of baked stuffed lobster. While he works he tells stories and listens to what I am doing with my life far away from home.

This visit instilled in me the knowledge that wherever I am, nearby a bear is loose in the woods. I need to shout, talk, and move about, or the bear will come and have his fun.

NO MORE HARNESS and track at home and no more harness and rolling platform at the rehab facility. It's just me with a gait belt around my waist, my walker, and a spotter. I can sit in a normal chair and then stand using the walker by pushing with my right hand off the chair arm. I can walk around the house without my wheelchair. It freaks me out. I over-grip the walker. This tension hinders my movement. I feel naked, out in space. It feels right despite the fear. When I stand, the muscles in my back yank and grip, screaming like a roller coaster pitching down. I am like Darwin's fish halfway between water and land. I'm practicing with a walker but I still use the wheelchair as my default way to get around.

We attach a raised seat with armrests to our toilet. Instead of being a wheeled performance-art exhibit, I can enter with my walker, drop my drawers, sit, pretend normality, read a magazine, and leave my gift with no help required. We equip our shower with a chair with adjustable legs. I manage the space using a grab bar and place my naked, skinny ass in a plastic seat, gripping anxiously to its sides. The seat has a back, handholds, and an inflatable cushion repurposed from camping geeks who like their comfort by the campfire. We can mothball my rolling bowel program and shower chair. It's a big step closer to a bedroom that looks like a bedroom and not a sickroom.

I'm upbeat until I go through the steps for a simple routine such as moving to the bed and sitting. My legs spasm as I scrunch my butt forward to the front of the wheelchair to stand up and take hold of my walker. I practice walking in place so I don't crash: step tense, step tense, back up to the bed, stick out my ass, and slowly sit. I walk from one end of the house to the other, conquer a ramp to a small porch, and sit in a plastic chair near the fishpond that was my before-the-fall obsession. I gaze at the view to the east. I see the Manzano Mountains, better than meditation.

My working frame of mind shifts perspective. As with most things that matter, there is no silver bullet—so patience is useful, given that I'm a physical mess, but the case is open for review. I know there is a light-a-match-to-the-dark philosophy because it is useful to ignore all that dark. Rage is handy in small doses, a safety valve for stuck spasms. In Ibsen's play *Peer Gynt*, the title character meets a shapeless creature, the Börg, which blocks his journey of self-discovery through the mountains. It whispers, "Go round!" until he solves its puzzle: not around, but through. The creature says, "He was too strong, he had women behind him." My through-wisdom isn't a solo act. Friends come to dinner. I am not the odd guy at the end of the table in a self-propelled vehicle with a tray in his lap. I transfer to a regular dining room chair and reclaim my place at the table.

There still is that hole drilled in my pubic zone to fit a catheter into my bladder. Recently, I had an accident. Suddenly pee came out where nature intended. I stood up from the bed and, without asking "May I take a giant step," peed on the floor with catheter intact, a three-cherries-on-the-slots event. Am I ready to pee au naturel? All good if so, but it makes a new complication. A man with a zippered fly and standard-issue working legs can nip into the nearest convenience and let loose. If I ditch my catheter, my moves to let loose are not at all simple. Time to experiment. I pinch off the suprapubic tube to see if my body will repeat the trick. I feel like a blackjack player shoving a big stack of chips forward—I'm holding a risky hand and waiting for the dealer to play his cards.

I ASK MY SURGEON, "Will I ever be free of spasticity?"

"Probably not," is the quick answer. He explains there are upper and lower systems that send nerve messages. The lower system is lodged in the limbs and sends out messages from the branching nerves that forest the muscles. In a normal body, the upper system, designed to control, suppresses any extra nerve messages or noise from the lower system so they don't get through to create uncontrolled movement or spasticity. This extra noise makes your leg feel fiery-prickly, and it builds up until it sets off a muscle to repeatedly contract. Workout junkies know what it is like to push through effort that is painful, and they revel in the willpower to manage it. Gain the conditioning and gain the pleasure of feeling fit and energized. In the wording of my deal, they left out the pleasure clause, or if it's there, it's mixed with yowling nerves that don't know how to ride the spinal bus without kicking a shin or digging a knuckle into a shoulder.

I have slyboots dreams. I am walking, like the man I was pre-fall. At the same time, I know I shouldn't be able to do this. But I am, and off I go. The wish is the dream.

I think, "This isn't so hard." Then my channel finder clicks to me in bed. The announcer says, "No, dummy. Not real. Clap for Tinkerbell and see if that helps."

How do I operate differently now? A point of comparison is time. There is the time it takes me to do things that once were quick: typing on my computer, picking up a paper from my desk, finding a document in a file, going to my bookcase for a book, and putting a check in an envelope. Then there is the time it takes to move in the wider world: waiting for a driver, navigating with a walker, and calculating how to do simple tasks like paying for coffee, stashing my wallet, then managing a hot coffee cup. Time feels thick, something I navigate through, rather than race. Time goes by just as fast as always, but there are fewer grab handles, so it feels as if it is always moving away from me. It is a little bit like what happens to time when you are sick with the flu.

Is there a more in-the-moment, Zen feature to my relationship to time? Isn't that supposed to be something that comes with the wisdom of being an elder? I haven't learned that. There is something different because time thickens and recedes. Trudging behind my walker automatically separates me from the flow of the ordinary world. That added bit of separation causes me to see it pass by, creatures riding folly's timeline, unaware, as I gaze on ruefully. So it is different from sitting in the coffee shop on the boulevard, watching the passing parade and enjoying its color and dazzle—that experience is a tonic for being part of that human parade. My body sets up a rhythm of small-to-large agitations that, as yet, has not allowed me to embrace the slowing of my human race. I strain against the sticky pace that often makes me feel like a flickering TV signal. Sometimes I'm fully seen; other times I blink off, invisible to those walking by.

What does it all mean, anyway? It's not a question but a condition. Look at your contract under Old Age, or Random Catastrophe, or Don't Blame the Management (we had nothing to do with it); see the addendum in the file marked J for Job; see codicil number zed stroke deuce stroke omega dash squash-like-bug. It's in the fine print. Of course shit happens. But so does bliss. The deal is, if you get bliss, you take your chances with getting pole-axed. It's part of the beat of time, backed by the All Hell Will Rain Down Orchestra. You just don't know when it will play. We sign the deal because we don't want to be still, don't want to hide in the dark; instead, we want to boogie in the light. We see and gape at beauty; we laugh, our bodies bent over or thrown back; we swagger and yell; we heave ourselves across the finish line, arms lifted or heads cast down. We know the bargain is irrevocable, carries no guarantees, and that the assignment of blame is unreliable.

When friends encounter me, I'm a big, shiny object. It is easy to forget that there is someone they don't see—Jennifer—who does a hundred things for me each day. Her part in keeping our story boat afloat without getting swamped and flipped over began as soon as we were tied together. We stood up in public and said so. Around us, storms formed in the unstable atmosphere fueled by our efforts to knit three boys, jangled by divorce and engaged in bouts of tribal warfare, into a family. Could our wedded craft, newly hammered and nailed, its hull cutting through breaking waves, survive? Before our stand-up-and-vow day, the boys had been below deck, saucy pirates taking axes to the planking, trying to sink the alien craft. It's different after they witness the do-you-take-to-love-and-cherish promise. No sleight of hand; everyone is dealt in. Our craft is beached, turned into a home. They are players with us in the story. Outside are cornfields, ditches to raft in, and the two of us playing out the newly-married pageant with its parade floats: see our garden grow; happy homemakers of America; and the boys' entry, let's raise hell when they're not looking. It's all so American every-family: a county fair, different exhibits, some rides scarier than others, and the odd prize for the perfect pig or rose.

Jennifer is made of flint, heart, and energy. She is a sauce that will burst into flame if you pour it on your bread and strike a match. She moves to stay ahead of the shadow of a mother who never embraced her. If you are in her care, it is indefatigable and unwavering. She takes delight in breaking rules, is unimpressed with excuses, and will kiss you till you faint if she loves you. She doesn't know the word "relax." She is incapable of coming home after work or shopping and just plunking down with a glass of wine to take a break. You'll never find a dirty dish sitting on her counter overnight. Her dogs think she is the prime mover in their creation myth, the source of good. There is no ready answer to the catastrophe that I brought into our lives with my accident. There is only seeing it as a new given in our story. This chapter, with both of us retired, is supposed to be the part when I will remove a few of the garments that dress her in duty for the obvious pleasure. Traveling the scenic wonders of the west in a rented road-hog of an RV has dropped off our to-do list. We're back in the writers' room, figuring out how the new given will reveal character.

One way it upends me is that my body and its skin are like a videogame that I can't seem to win. I want to think my progression will be more or less a straight line. Now each day when I wake up, I'm in some new zone of combat and discovery. One day it's spasms in the legs after supper, my chest clamping up like a vise; another day it's shortness of breath with tight shoulders, rigid left arm thrown in randomly. One day I pop up like a jack rabbit, ready to go, and yet on another I'm stuck in molasses—no rabbit, hands cold or thick and fat, and so on. If only there were a controller in this shooter game I'd fight back more directly. I'd earn powers and fight my way to smooth ground, clear skies, and loose limbs. What doesn't change is that the body is the environment for our feelings as we start each day, formed anew from our nightly wrestle with desire and fear.

I stand, holding onto nothing, and close my eyes, making little adjustments of my hands to keep my balance. I raise my left hand in front of my face, bent a bit sideways at the elbow. The mini ice age slowly releases my shoulder. I walk holding Colleen's forearms, stepping through, my foot not clumping like a Halloween cartoon monster or bent to the left. I can pull my pants down and back up in the privacy of my bathroom, getting there on my own from chair to walker to seat. It's good to know I can break some law out in public should I be seized with the crazy.

Another poke in the eye of character is the conflict between voices. One voice says, "Run for the cheese: this way, that way, do more." The other voice says, "Not sure about cheese, really hard to do, who needs it, maybe tomorrow." The voices scrape against each other like fingernails on a chalkboard. Pleasure is a power. The trick is, who's the boss of pleasure?

Thanksgiving arrives with another chance to test how my new-given circumstance pulls at the thread of my character. The day is a chance for a new memory with no need for hiding in my it's-all-about-me closet. Can I avoid the part of a dim bulb that casts little light beyond my precious suffering-man shade? When I wake in the morning I am weepy. Activity is happening all around me in my house, but I am like some free radical, feeling the absence of something. All our children are gathering at Matt's house in Los Angeles. Matt, his wife Amy, and their daughter Isabel are hosting Hadrian, Jason, and their families. It is show time in Matt and Amy's first house; here they are, a couple with a mortgage. Our grandchildren are at Matt's new table in California; Jennifer and I are at the table their parents knew as children. We are hosting a group of friends in Albuquerque. Our group could be a little United Nations, with Russian, French, Dutch, and some Polish come to parlay over Pilgrim turkey and pumpkin pie. Jennifer plays general to the troops in the kitchen, gives her heart to the feast, and grooves her own new memory line. In hers, I'm no longer bustling here and there setting up tables, making fires, lifting the turkey in and out of the oven, sharpening my grandfather's bone-handled knife, and carving the bird. Friends are helping, and she loves presiding over the coming together at the table. Decommissioned from the officer corps, I am an observer, and socialize. I also do a job I've always done: write a toast. This Thanksgiving is a bookend. The years 2008 and 2012 are the election and reelection of Barack Obama, the bookends of his two campaigns. He has the O in mojo, going two for two. I'm surprised at how this extraordinarily decent man's defeat of the worst instincts of our body politic gives lift to my personal agenda of hope. All seated. They stare at their mashed potatoes, waiting. I stay out of the poor-me closet, hit a button on my mental jukebox, and deliver my toast.

I feel O's hope. He did it; no bullshit. I allow that victory to float, even though the evidence for my own situation tells me I'm in a lottery. We have a lottery ticket that says we have two years. Like Lazarus, I'm a quadriplegic that stands up, a spazoid that walks medium distances in physical therapy gripping an assistive device. I have usable arms, one pretty good and another not, and a return-to-the-factory sense of balance. I can undress myself without help. My spasms are fewer. Why? No clue. I can butter my toast, cut my meat, and drink my milk. I'm a beat up seven-year-old with a good vocabulary. I work, teach a course, go about in the world in a wheelchair, and socialize with friends. The clock is running on year two.

MY ADRENALINE SPIKES whenever I start to walk. Will I fall over on my ass? My left leg is in spasm; I thought walking would stop it. A spasm shoots my leg up and kicks me over backward. My head thwacks the floor; the hardware inside my neck holds firm. I hit the meltdown switch. I'm scared and think regression. A little gnashing and whining clears the sinus. Luckily, the young man who drives me arrives. I'm an agitated, anxious mess until we figure out how to pick me up. Rolling over on all fours is not a skill yet. I'm too much dead weight. It takes a chair. Step one, I'm moved so my back is against the chair seat. Step two, I'm lifted into the chair. Step three, I'm helped to stand and grip my walker. Step four, stop the curses and feeling sorry for myself.

What if change stops? What if it continues, but it doesn't feel any better than it does now? What if my nerves never let me be comfortable in my skin? Jennifer doesn't want to hear these gloomy thoughts. How is our story changing? Here is a new scene. Jennifer has been hard at work all day watering, doing laundry, and putting clean sheets on the bed. She's at the sink washing a dish with extra energy, and is extra quiet. I come into the kitchen and ask, "What's the matter?"

Her first move is to say, "I don't want to talk about it."

I counter with, "It's no good if we don't talk when we're upset." Depending on how pissed she is, we get to the heart of the matter next. The more pissed she is, the longer she stays cocooned in silence. Soon it comes out. She's discouraged and upset. She's working hard, covering for my absent ass, and I'm not working on my body hard enough. Too much sitting. I have lists of exercises I can be doing. She doesn't see me doing any. I'm distant. I don't seem interested in touching her, giving her a hug. I'm always in my head. She knows that's who I am, but I have to work harder or I won't get any better. She knows this; she's been a body person all her life. I feel ambushed because I think I am working hard and I'm sick to death of the battle with my spasms and my whacked-out body. I feel trapped; I can't be honest about expressing my doubts without hurting her. When I hurt, or get upset, I raise my voice. She feels I'm shouting at her. Sometimes I'm quiet and apologize, which doesn't help. I know she's right: I can work harder. Her fire hose on my Sleepy Jim act leaves no honest fig leaf. It's hard to explain why I don't even see the depression that I must climb over to do more physically. But I really don't want to make excuses, and she's not asking for them.

The scene runs out of steam. We hug. She's sorry for the ambush. I say I'll try harder. Sometimes I do. I mean it when I say it. She shifts into doing encouragement and we move on. These flame-ups are part of the story now. It is a tug of war for something real. We want the cheerleading and the push for more. A push is effective said once, encouragement leaves a choice, skepticism is a belief, not a fact. Two people can hold different beliefs.

One can say, "I know you believe that, but it upsets me to hear you say it." We each have our fantasy of what the world is, and our needs sometimes nestle together and sometimes bristle apart. No one gets to be monarch and declare their needs absolute. Time will deliver all the absolutes we can deal with.

Language likes to hide its intent. A friend points out that most questions are a lie. He starts with the Bible and points to God as a practiced liar. When God asks Cain, "Where is your brother?" God knows very well where he is. He knows he is dead by Cain's hand. The question isn't genuine. It isn't something that is the beginning of a way to talk. It is the beginning of a way to judge. When someone asks, "Have you done your exercises?" or "Is supper ready?" these questions aren't real either. They carry within them a judgment: why haven't you done them, why isn't it ready? You aren't doing enough. Can we find how to keep it simple? Light a flame, but leave a choice; state a preference, not a demand? In everyday life, simplicity and directness leave heart-space for the freewheeling beings we love and the stories that form around us.

DEAR DIARY, where does the wind blow? Think of the following as a diary entry recording my tumbled thoughts on how luck, therapy, and nature transformed regions of my fallow anatomy before the bank foreclosed on my two-year spinal cord mortgage. What happens in the second year of the most critical period for return of function? There is more to the story I want to tell. Whatever state my body is in, I still have a life to live. This is more complicated than physical rehabilitation. The question—how to live—is a question to ask and not avoid. If chance scribbles over the story of who I am as a physical and emotional being, only I can rewrite it.

By now I know a few things. I'm more than a big veg-etable for others to work with as raw material. In April 2013, a production of *The Menu*, drawn from my col-lection of poems, opens in a theater and plays for three weeks. We find life outside of trips to rehab and clean-ing catheter bags. Jennifer and I work with the cast in rehearsal. She works with stage movement and I huddle with the director as she imagines how to dramatize my poetry. This is how we met and began fooling around. Rehearsal isn't sex, but it is pleasure: it pumps life into rusty art skills. My book of poems traces a loose narra-tive of how I came to understand the shape of life, the place of love, the force of need, and the fragility of happi-ness. It's a mouthful! I hope it's true.

We like sex; we're just not getting any of the coupling kind right now. It's listed in the two-year mortgage as, "Unavailable, return date TBA." I have bad days and don't want to do crap. It gets worse. I dream the big fix is just around the corner. Go ahead, sell me desert land in Arizona a hundred miles from an electric light. I think pleasure is on a lot of people's minds, don't you? With-out it there are no art students or art schools. Someone has to know about the needs of the flesh, feelings, beauty, and rhythm and blues, unless all you care about is the industrial model brain with stick shift, straight eight, and a radio that plays only the sports stations. The bor-ders between pleasure and denial don't show clearly on any map. My effort is like map-making, a re-inhabiting of lost territory. I say we want it hard and we want it soft and everything in between. Art can help with that.

I'm thinking in Pearl Harbor-sized headlines: MAN LEAVES WHEELCHAIR. CAUSE DEBATED. NO PREACHER IN SIGHT. I meet Hugo, a brand of roll-ing walker. The name in script is printed on the front.

I'm ready to smell the mothballs and find space in the storeroom to exile my power chair unit. I make the switch from wheelchair to walker. It's like dieting; I cut down a little at a time. I move around the house with no wheelchair. I go from my desk chair to a dining room chair to a family room chair. Faint applause as I take laps around the kitchen island while Jennifer cooks. Better yet, I swing my legs up onto our elliptical trainer. I huff and puff, count as the minutes tick off to thirteen and the step readout says 700. Hugo's frame is blue with a black seat that lifts to store more than a mother's purse. I try it out on a walk up the ramp to my van, stoop beneath the doorframe, and walk backward to sit in the rear seat. "Town, Jeeves." Hugo is also the name of the kid in the Martin Scorsese movie of the same name. He is pursued by an obsessed gendarme, bent on arresting him for thieving in the train station. The kid lives in a large station clock. I live bound by a clock, so the walker has the right name. The spasm attacks that stalk and beat me just because they can are my obsessed gendarme. The walker means I've conquered territory thought abandoned, a not-so-little victory moment. Cue the girl who'll kiss the soldier. I discover I stop traffic as effectively as a *Sports Illustrated* swimsuit model by creeping over a crosswalk slower than the traffic light countdown.

I stop writing about my progress. I'd kept up my weekly reports on changes and describing how it feels to be the me of me and the me of Jennifer. A large circle of friends and colleagues checks in to this serial tale. My friends wonder if my absence means I've thrown in the towel or taken to drink. My retirement fuss recently happened. I close the door on a thirty-eight-year career at the University of New Mexico. Perhaps rehearsal, enacting the tribal rite of retirement, the burning of incense, the speechmaking, the gathering of friends, all overwhelmed my obsessive blah, blah, blah about my body. I don't want to talk any more about the topic of my damned body. Yes, the wheelchair is gone. Thanks for the memories, I guess. I'm not bounding around the house like a gazelle. Instead, it's more of a slo-mo scene with legs that feel waterlogged and subject to junkyard-dog spasms. I'm doing all my therapies. I'm sick up to my eyeballs of my story. But despite that, the walker-enabled version of reality gives me just enough independence from the wheelchair version that it changes how I think about myself. I've stepped out of the door of the sick room. I can feel the bit-of-more between my teeth.

WTF! I am physically stronger, but still both my legs buckle. I keel over backward at home, smack! I'm on my back like a turtle flipped over by a mean kid, legs and arms wiggling in the air. This time Jennifer and I don't hit the panic button. Thanks to Colleen and Pilates I can pull my trunk onto an end table, rest on my knees, then draw my right leg up. With my foot on the floor, I push my butt into the seat of my walker. It is a high five, and then a middle finger to the bitch of bad fortune.

ABOUT A YEAR after my accident, Craig Hospital sends me a recall notice. They want to know what I've made of myself since they last saw me. Can we stand going back? Jennifer, not so much. But she drives me there, armored with a good friend, Eric Newton, also a former professional dancer. He comes along to keep Jennifer distracted with trips to IKEA while Craig staff pokes and prods the recalled merchandise. I'm pinching off my catheter to coax my bladder into full-time regular service. Our drive is measured out by pee stops for my bladder, which acts like an out-of-shape prima donna in spring training.

I arrive as the student you hated in school who wants to show off his homework. Look at me: a walker, no wheelchair, *check*; no mechanical lift, *check*; no rolling shower chair, *check*; feed and dress without help, *check*; get in and out of bed with no assist, *check*. I want a gold star, damn it! Walking through the door into the hospital, I feel like the butterfly must feel toward the caterpillar. At every appointment there is a moment of wide-eyed recognition that such change has occurred in a little over a year's time. Dr. Skelza, who leads my evaluation team, keeps his cool and doesn't shout out, "You're awesome!" He does something just as good: he says, "Let's bring him back for an upgrade." What I hear is, "Let's fix him. He's ready." I want them to figure out how to construct a stabilizer, perhaps some fancy new fins, reengineering me to sleek. I watch people walk the way I looked at cars as a teenager, grading their cool. The upgrade session can last for two weeks to work on my new abilities. They'll decide by the end of my recall evaluation.

At the recall, I feel like the odd duck among all the patients in wheelchairs. My physical difference from my previous time at Craig works like a shield against harsh memories. They give me a balance test. What can I do? Try to stand on one foot and tap a block with the free foot without holding onto something. Try to reach down and pick something off the floor without holding on. Try to rise up on my toes, eyes closed, and many more such things that I can't remember. Out of a possible fifty-six points on my balance test, I score a twenty-nine. I am summoned to the gait clinic on the first day, to a group of bright-looking people holding clipboards. I might think I'm in Victor Frankenstein's lab, if my observers were not so young, Colorado fresh, and empathetic that the comparison is unhinged. They ask me to take a lap around the room with my walker and follow me like ducklings. I can tell they are happy with what they see, as they chat about my left foot and my right knee. Next they take away my walker and give me two cuff crutches. Because my shoulder is stiff, my left arm is awkward. They swap my left crutch for a cane. I move around the room tapping my crutch and my cane to sounds of approval. They try a brace to keep my right knee from hyperextending. They try a device to keep my left foot straighter. They are the gait gadget people. Colleen, my Pilates therapist, has come up to see what she can learn from the Craigheads. She is watching the gait show. I can feel the gears turning in her head. She thinks we should fix the muscles and alignment before relying on a mechanical device.

After the gait clinic, I go to the zero gravity track. This is the fancy version of what we did on our porch with an overhead track, me in a vest and a rope between. They put on the vest and say, "Let's see how you walk without anything." I creep along, shoulders tensed, not trusting my balance. They give me the crutch and the cane and I walk with more confidence. I am a project, a fixer-upper. I'm sent to the bladder people. They scan and find some bladder stones. News to me.

At the final recall conference the upgrade invite is made: a two-week plan that can extend or shorten. Jennifer and Colleen think, "Well, they'll ask us any second now. How did you do it? What did you do? Give us the highlights." I'm the only patient I see walking without a wheelchair. I can't be the only one who has an incomplete injury. But the recall conference ends without a question asked of us. Craigites pat me on the back for my character. Character is supposed to make everyone feel good and will cover the gap. It is the I-don't-want-to-really-know answer.

Before we go out the door they say, "Wait, there's a catch about the upgrade." My invite to the upgrade dance requires that I have no suprapubic catheter tube sticking into my bladder. Oh, and those bladder stones. Take care of them. I can pee fine during the day with the catheter tied off. I don't know how to get through the night. There is a small pond of pee in my night catch bag in the morning. How am I going to get through the night if I have to pee that much? I'll be a jack-in-the-box, up peeing all the time. OK, OK, I'd actually like to unstrap the pee bag and go au naturel. I like to sleep, too, but fine, no suprapubic catheter tube, no stones.

Back home. Step one, remove bladder stones, *check*. Let me count the ways to pee at night. I try a condom catheter; no go. Then I try to swing my legs over the edge of the bed and pee into a capture vessel; no go. Next I try a portable, stand-alone pee pot next to the bed. This last option I can manage. It goes like this: I fall asleep until I'm harshly jerked awake as my bladder causes my whole body to spasm. My knees are yanked to my chest as my arms shoot out straight. I have to force my legs out straight or they will cramp. This is the gentle nudge my bladder uses to tell me I need to pee. It's as if my bladder owns a Taser. I struggle to stand, grunting and groaning so I get karmic credit, look at the clock, and swear, as it's barely an hour since I fell asleep. I stand, grip the walker, shuffle, pivot, back up a few steps, pull down my drawers, sit, wait, relax, pee. This goes on. Then one night, groggy and trying to pull down my pajama bottoms, I stick my hand in between my gut and the suprapubic tube, then grab my drawers and push down. My hand yanks down my pajama bottoms, and also yanks the suprapubic tube out of my belly. Pee gushes out of the hole where the suprapubic tube used to be, splashing on the floor at my feet. Well, that solves the problem of getting rid of my suprapubic. Way to go, Houdini. You've freed yourself. No more tube. Gone.

What did I do? Is this a 911 moment? There's no blood (not much, anyway) and no pain. I remember my urologist saying, "We just pull it out; the hole heals on its own. We cover it with a pad for leaks until it heals. It takes maybe two weeks and zippity-do-dah, good as new." But now I have the swell experience of leaking from the freed hole. Two weeks pass and it is not sealed closed. Two months later, the doctor gets out his needle and thread. Add that I am in the land of sleep deprivation until my bladder figures out it can hold it past an hour without a hysterical, fainting Taser fit. Waking up every hour wreaks havoc with REM sleep. This gets old fast. My bladder has been on vacation at the beach for a year and is not happy to go back to work. It's too used to emptying without thinking, without working its muscle, a hopeless couch potato. I need it to *do its job*! It sulks and resists. It makes me a puppet of its whims at night for months. That's a lot of karmic groaning for Jennifer to hear. I try different medicines to help the bladder relax, but finally it is just time that does the trick. The bladder on good behavior means I'm up usually four times a night, with the occasional lapse into bad old ways. I dream again.

I'm fine during the day. No embarrassing moments, no searching for a bathroom as in the endless TV ads. No special underwear. But what idiots design bathroom doors? A majority are solid, heavy doors with gorilla-strength closer mechanisms. My arm strength at this time is such that I can just manage crumpling a sheet of paper. The reason that bathrooms have solid, hard-to-open doors is because . . . ? When I try to muscle my way in, some people notice and help, others notice and don't. Most bathrooms have a handicapped stall. Nearly all have grab bars, but some, remarkably, do not. Toilets are some standard height that you are completely used to when lowering your precious bum. My toilet at home has a raised seat with armrests on each side that helps with the up from down. The lower I go, the harder it is to get my weight over my feet to stand. I need something to pull against to hoist my skinny butt up into *Homo erectus*. Visiting friends' houses poses a variety of contortional problems of how to lever up and away from the great convenience. Oh my God, listen to me! Such bitching and whining for what others with my injury would kill to have. Bladder and bowel function is a great leap ahead, period. It doesn't matter how long it took, or what troubles I have to outsmart, I now have the gold standard for normalcy and independence. How about an orgasm? I'm waiting, but there I go again.

LIKE READERS of a fairy tale, Jennifer and I are anxious for what comes next, for this new time when neither of us will be teaching. Is there some creature that must be tricked, a spell undone, or task accomplished that will take us out of these tangled woods? Our dreams race ahead to travel and the sights. My body reacts to the thought of new adventures: *"What? Ah, maybe. I guess. (Shoulder shrug.) Not sure. It all depends. (Brow furrows.) Maybe."* Where's our hero? So the Nike ad doesn't apply to real life? He's chicken and has to talk himself into what is not familiar. Jennifer must love that. She's ready to pack her bags. Our hero mostly does come around, but has to work the logistics, like moving large, breakable freight. Whatever will come, it will come with a bill of particulars and a cost. The management can say, "We've done everything we can, pay up, and don't give us that look, you ingrate. You can think about your needs all you want. They never will be met." Artist codicil: "Ha, ha, call the fool to distract you. Step up, the play runs only once, hold love close so the heart won't freeze."

My friends react by making me a character in a story. There is a well-worn narrative that descends on those stricken by injury. The person they knew is lost, out of sight, and out of reach. People touch me and praise my progress. I'm conflicted by the praise. I also know I represent something more than that character. I represent something like a spiritual relic. Embedded in my struggle is a value that we want to believe exists. It is the desire to see a fight against a fall, triumph over surrender. We want the grit and the madness. We want the story where we hurl ourselves against misfortune, where we crush doubt. Then anything can happen; we walk free, our shoulders squared. We want to see the body get up, stand up. We want struggle, then failure, and then, slowly, something wonderful. Those who throw down their crutches collect a prize; better than the enormous panda with a red ribbon, we endow their innards with special sauce. Their character is greater. We don't know what the hell it is, but we're glad we don't have to show it to get through our day. It must be something like spirit or courage. Each story is idiosyncratically different, but generically the same. Life won't be suppressed. It will fight against the forces that make the body a prison. The body may be caged, but the spirit can fly. (See Stephen Hawking or Christopher Reeve, and countless others whose names we don't know.)

This story has the power to carry the fallen forward and shore up the belief that they can reverse the mischief of chance. I cling to it as to a life raft. It feeds on its own energy, fueled by supporters: those who love me, friends who admire my efforts, and those I don't want to disappoint. The brain needs the mini hero-drama of struggling to beat the odds to help fence off the pain and avoid surrendering to despair and bitterness. Left by myself— with my junkyard body and the outsized efforts required to move, to gain strength when little fireflies of nerve and muscle connections flash—I might not try. But I'm a creature in a glass cage, watched and cheered on by many, and I use that breath to fan the flames.

Eventually the brain's battle to overcome the trouble it's in must come to an end; you either conquer your territory or you don't. But my battle isn't one that can have a black-and-white victory. I'll end up on a continuum somewhere between the wreck that I became and the whole person I once was. The suspense is where on that continuum I can push myself to. Ultimately, damage is damage, and will have its say.

CHAPTER FIVE

The Bear and I

IT WILL BE DONE, over and done, whatever is won. Who's the judge? Check the price. Are returns allowed, with no questions asked, if he doesn't last? Lock the door, give him the bill. He owes us a thrill.

The truth is, we live beyond this dog-eared story, wherever it takes us. Whatever we become, we learn the story ends, but time does not. We live in new circumstances for the long run, however far that may be. Looking beyond the Dropped On His Head season series, I can't help but know it's a fraction of what defines the human condition. The thrill of gaining some advantage after being mauled by chance shouldn't blind us with happy talk about victories, or end in the moral All Things Are Possible. After a career in the theater, I can't look away from all the human need squeezed in the vise of an indifferent world, a view that finds its elemental expression in Samuel Beckett.

In 1961 I was in college, trying to understand the different powers of my dick and my brain, along with the mystery of my heart caught between them. Beckett's *Happy Days*, published the same year, imagines a middle-aged couple, Winnie and Willie, trapped by these same forces. It strips away pretense, showing the way our paths in life are defined by blunted desire and terrible heartbreak. Beckett's unflinching vision of the dark night beneath humanity's ceaseless stories of hope and need for love offers an asymmetry that matches the experience of those who are tripped up by random chance. The scene that opens the play shows no room with table and chairs, or any domestic space or garden setting, but the metaphorical landscape of existence. It is a landscape that can be understood by those whose bodies have been knocked down and thieved by blind chance.

> *Expanse of scorched grass rising center to low mound. Gentle slopes down to front to either side of stage.*
> . . .
> *Blazing light.*
>
> . . . *Unbroken plain and sky receding to meet in far distance.*
>
> *Imbedded up to above her waist in exact center of mound, WINNIE. About fifty, well preserved. Blond for preference, plump, arms and shoulders bare, low bodice, big bosom, pearl necklet. She is discovered sleeping, her arms on the ground before her, her head on her arms.*
> . . .
> *To her right and rear, lying asleep on ground, hidden by mound, WILLIE.*
>
> A bell rings repeatedly like an alarm and wakes Winnie. Her first words are:
>
> (*Gazing at zenith*). Another heavenly day.

She continues in excruciating prosaic detail: she brushes her teeth, calls to Willie and ruminates on him, inspects her teeth and gums in a hand mirror, thinks more on how Willie "can sleep forever," finds spectacles, takes out handkerchief and polishes them, ruminates on sight, examines print on toothbrush, remarks on her headaches, calls to Willie, picks up parasol, taps Willie with parasol, drops it, Willie returns it, cautions Willie not to go off, examines color of her palms—takes revolver from bag, kisses it, puts it back, reads label on a red medicine bottle for—"Lack of spirits," takes a swig, finds lipstick—"low," does lips, Willie's bald head appears trickling blood, covers his head with handkerchief, settles boater on head— "rakish angle," tells Willie to dress, announces—"Oh this is going to be another happy day."

Willie is largely hidden behind the mound, except for a view of his head; we see his arm when he reads a newspaper or a postcard. She treats her condition as the way things are, a given, the way the world is. Winnie, immobilized below her waist, has only her mind to fill the silence. Through some primal intuition we accept this scene and focus on what emotional world emerges in this bleak landscape. The existential ferocity of her condition haunts her dialogue as an undertow that breaks out in fretful speech. Their interaction is the banal conversation of couples. Willie reads want ads and obituaries from a newspaper: "His Grace and Most Reverend Father in God Dr. Carolus Hunter dead in tub." Winnie reminisces, "My first ball! (*Long pause.*) My second ball! (*Long pause. Closes eyes.*) My first kiss!"

Her hold on happiness is made of ordinary things that bridge to final things. She deciphers the words on her toothbrush that say what its bristles are made of and connects the joy of learning new things with that day when no more pain is possible, when one is no longer flesh. The simultaneous presence of joy, pain, and thoughts of death's release is a familiar consciousness to the afflicted, even though Beckett makes no distinction. He sees everyone so afflicted.

And if for some strange reason no further pains are possible, why then, just close the eyes—(*she does so*)—and wait for the day to come—(*opens eyes*)—the happy day to come when flesh melts and the night of the moon has so many hundred hours.

We feel Winnie's bond with Willie is what allows her to continue. At the beginning of Act II, Beckett ups the ante.

Winnie is buried to her neck in the mound. Willie has been absent. How much must be taken away before a person no longer throws light against loss? She cannot turn or raise or lower her head. She faces front; just her eyes move. If we expect that the change has dashed her spirits and thrown her into a black mood, we would be wrong.

Hail, holy light. (*Long pause. She closes her eyes. Bell rings loudly. She opens her eyes at once. Bell stops. She gazes front. Long smile. Smile off. Long pause.*) Someone is looking at me still. Caring for me still. That is what I find so wonderful.

Winnie's emotion stirs and deepens as her condition worsens. Near the close of the act she has not seen Willie. Different thoughts crowd into her mind. She wonders how she can go on, but something must move and she no longer can. She then tries to recall the appropriate words.

What are those immortal lines? (*Pause.*) It might be the eternal dark. (*Pause.*) Black night without end. (*Pause.*) Just chance, I take it, happy chance. (*Pause.*) Oh yes, abounding mercies.

The play's final moments begin when Willie appears.

WILLIE'S head appears to her right round corner of mound. He is on all fours, dressed to kill—top hat, morning coat,

> *striped trousers, etc., white gloves in hand. Very long bushy*
> *Battle of Britain moustache.*

Willie struggles, crawling on all fours to reach Winnie. Winnie vacillates between wondering where he has been, if he means to stay, does he want to touch her face, keeps encouraging him to come to her as Willie strains up, moves and falters. Her encouragement suggests it is for intimate contact, then when she asks him to look at her she is surprised at what she sees. When he speaks, it is just her name, "Win." Still buried up to her neck, Winnie claims this faltering, straining scrap of connection as progress, and she begins to sing.

. . .

> *Every touch of fingers*
> *Tells me what I know,*
> *Says for you,*
> *It's true, it's true,*
> *You love me so!*

Beckett stands witness for those who don't want to tell a false tale of heroism or deny the knowledge that human life can be a blessing wrapped in a curse. Our job is to not tell lies about what it takes to prop up our happiness on the tender shoots of small mercies, holding our gaze upward, away from: "It might be the eternal dark. Black night without end." The great British writer, Harold Pinter, explained in a letter to a friend why Beckett was an essential voice for him:

> He is the most courageous, remorseless writer going and the more he grinds my nose in the shit the more I am grateful to him. He's not fucking me about, he's not leading me up any garden path, he's not slipping me a wink, he's not flogging me a remedy or a path or a rev-

elation or a basinful of breadcrumbs, he's not selling me anything I don't want to buy—he doesn't give a bollock whether I buy or not—he hasn't got his hand over his heart. Well, I'll buy his goods, hook, line and sinker, because he leaves no stone unturned and no maggot lonely . . .

UPGRADE READY! I am in a Winnie frame of mind. Each day buried in this body is a happy day. I arrive at Craig without a suprapubic catheter and without bladder stones. Jennifer can't face another day at this hospital and stays home. I'm here with my driver, Caroline, who'll double as my helper. I'm anticipating what new thing might come of this trip. I'm thinking, "Christmas." Craig is thinking, "Test and measure, observe, maybe we can raise some ability a notch or find a better adaptation." I'm the kid who thinks he's getting a pony and they're the parents who buy practical clothes for school.

My original therapists, Caitlin and Meghan, are no longer doing their old jobs. Meghan has a title on her door and is running a new experimental program. Caitlin, now a Mrs., is working with brain injury patients. I miss the laughs and the high beams and the I-dare-you moments. On my recall visit we have a pizza together at a table in an outside area of the hospital. We share you're-doing-really-great looks and look-what's-happened fist bumps. It is my turn to mess with them. I tell them I'm writing a book and describe our first meeting, when they said to me, "Get your lazy ass out of bed, you faker." They shriek and for the tiniest moment believe me.

This time I'll be with new therapists at the outpatient wing. As before, I have OT and PT sessions each day. They know I have idle time and show me how to use different exercise equipment in the gymnasium, where another Rocky Mountain High girl gives me the don't-be-a-putz look with her light-the-dark smile and invites me to come hang out and break a sweat. The gait gurus have first crack at me with my new PT. They decide I don't need any prosthetic devices for my left leg. They think I should work on using cuff crutches. The PT works me out on cuff crutches off and on during the upgrade. We crutch on different terrain inside and outside the hospital: grass, curbs, gravel, and ramps. She is able to put me on the zero gravity track a couple times. On the track, the mind really wants to say, "I got this. Just walk on out the way you have all your life." But I still need a U.N.'s worth of translators between wish and act as I'm tense, more lurching like a crab than walking.

Craig has a new toy called a vibration plate. The device migrated from elite sports into the therapy arena. It looks like a large scale. There are controls at the top of a center post, and the bottom is a large oval, wider than the size of a chair seat. The plate vibrates at different intensities and times. When you put your body on it, the vibration recruits nerves and muscles to connect. The sports world says it creates the equivalent of a full workout in a matter of minutes and tunes the muscles up a notch. I stand on it for a short warm-up vibration. Then the PT has me put my forearms on the plate, with my feet stretched out in a plank position. I am vibrated for just thirty seconds and it knocks the stuffing out of me. Craig makes no claims about this experiment. Serious long-term research has yet to be published on the device. The jocks don't think it has a lasting effect. But for spazmeisters that may not be the final story.

I am puzzled, then miffed, that Craig's research arm has zero interest in my recovery from quadriplegic to ambulatory with a walker. I talk to a quantitative researcher, who hands me off to a qualitative researcher. Neither is curious about what I did: my Pilates work with Colleen, cranial acupuncture, or the walking track at home. They only ask if my gains happened in the predicted two-year frame of recovery. When I say yes their eyes glaze over. They are so blinkered by their timeline that there is no flicker of curiosity. It doesn't occur to them that a collection of recovery stories, no matter how idiosyncratic, would be very useful to those challenged by spinal cord injuries. Their indifference presents itself as arrogance about methodology: they can't be bothered to ask for any details of my recovery. News to me that I should've sat on my ass and just let the magic of time make me better. I left thinking this was intellectual laziness masquerading as science.

Matt comes to visit on the middle weekend of my upgrade. We spend the day driving to Boulder, where he spent two years at the university. It has been some time since we were alone together just to talk. Boulder is nostalgia territory. It takes him back to his first years away from home. Matt's a talker. Father and son alone, the talk isn't about sports. What's a father anyway? One of the hardest parts of my divorce was leaving this little boy in the lurch when I walked out of the marriage. One need crushed another; there's no prettying up this picture. Time with Matt was shared on a schedule, but he was left to fend for himself with his mother. She could be critical and invest in conflict with intense mental energy, creating looping, exhausting, argumentative confrontations. She was a walking weather system with a permanent storm-warning alert attached. Matt was only six when I left. He learned emotional survival skills in the wake of my exit. Jennifer and I didn't get married until he was eleven. It was no picnic for Hadrian and Jason, either. The time with their father was more random, but they had Jennifer. When any of the boys talk about this period, I think I am about to be brought before the bench to answer for my sins.

None of this is on Matt's mind. Instead, he is poking me about not paying enough attention to his education. Jennifer and I are professors, yet he feels he had to work things out on his own. He's right. That's what we'd done; worked it out ourselves. Were we a cliché of the I-walked-five-miles-in-the-snow-so-shall-you variety? I remember standing in my parents' kitchen in Maine, telling my father about my interview for a teaching job at Tufts. I could tell my public lecture got mixed reviews. My father and I were in different worlds. He had sympathy, a good choice, but no way of knowing if my fears were justified. Matt and I are not in such different worlds. He graduated with a degree in English and film from UC Santa Cruz and eventually earned an MFA in film from Columbia. On the car ride we talk about when he dropped out of school to work for a national publication, *TransWorld SNOWboarding Magazine*. He was a sponsored snowboarder when they asked him to come work for them. He left school. He quickly realized his writing skills— mostly his lack of knowledge about grammar—made him stand out like Hawthorne's Hester Prynne with the scarlet letter *A*. Implied was: How did we let this happen? His discomfort led him to enroll in a writing/grammar course. Everything about the magazine job was seductive. It sent him around the world with pay, and he was in one of the cool hotspots of youth culture. After he'd spent a couple of years taking this ride, they offered him a top editing job at the magazine. He turned them down and went back to school. He'd figured out that for him the sports magazine world was the same thing over and over again, a niche with a small horizon.

Turning points provide chapter headings in life stories; circumstances lead to decisions that reveal the values that drive our lives. At this turning in Matt's life we had no son-and-dad chat about his choice. He sorted it out by himself, as Hadrian and Jason did with their own turning points. It seems to me the job of the father is to know when to shut up and when to stay away from yelling instructions as the kid in his or her rowboat is thrashed about by wind and will. A child's task is to separate from parents and learn to trust himself at such a turn. Parents are both close and far at the same time. Knowing this dynamic doesn't stop us questioning whether there could have been more: more contact and involvement, a more that is both why and why not.

I have turning-point stories, and on this ride Matt has shared one of his. I can take the rap for not paying enough attention in the past. He's earned his question to me and he's earned his success. Our talk is a sign of another upgrade. I'm a father that a son can poke and share with from his personal issue file. I've shed my mantle of sick man, damaged goods. Matt no longer has to tread carefully to avoid serious topics that stir feelings.

In the final week of my upgrade I ask to be checked out for driving. I feel like a teenager again. They lead me out to a car in the parking lot, open the driver's door, and tell me to put my foot on the accelerator, now shift it to the brake, now back and forth. My foot's ability to lift and turn is not within the margin of error. I keep bumping into the side of the brake pedal. They say, "Nice try, but no cigar."

My upgrade time is over. My Craig experience has run its course. They whittled a disaster down to something that is livable. They did it with skill, humor, patience, and knowledge, blended to face people when they're at their worst and slowly teach them to lift their eyes to the horizon. They helped me go where I wanted to go, once I was able to see beyond my misery. They never pretended a sow's ear was a silk purse, and they didn't say there was anything wrong with a sow's ear. I met remarkable people there; I'm grateful for what they taught me and the ways they helped me heal.

BACK HOME, a few months later, I am evaluated by a private outfit called Driving to Independence. For a fat check, they probe my mental powers, assess my knowledge of driving regulations and road situations, and take me on a long road test. I pass. They send my test results to New Mexico's Motor Vehicle Division, which in turn sends me a letter that officially approves me to drive over a ton of metal at lethal speeds on the state's roads. Instead of getting in the van by wheelchair ramp, I open the sliding door on the driver's side. With the door open, I tilt the front of my walker up so the front wheels roll onto the lowered floor of the van. I place the walker behind the driver's seat and attach a bungee cord around the walker to the handle on the back of the seat. I hoist my right leg onto the floor in front of the driver's seat and leverage my butt into the seat. Twisting around to grab the seatbelt, I wriggle myself into place and put the key in the ignition.

AS HAPPY AS I AM with the function that's come back and with hope for more, I don't have excited anticipation for things to come. The broken feeling in my body is relentless, despite my ability to do the moves in Pilates and my gains in independence. The feeling is better than it was, but I'm more vulnerable to it. Before, I could adopt the new-warrior-in-combat stance. Now the long haul is visible. So what is it, Captain Ahab, the whale not so thrilling anymore?

In her book *Brain on Fire*, Susannah Cahalan describes how in the heat of her nightmare, when her mental world began to collapse, her father kept asking, "What is the slope of the line?" The answer he always wanted to hear was "up." In her case, this became true. I think the slope of my line is up. How much more, is the question. Unlike Susannah's story, there is no medical mystery about what caused my condition. But there is a mystery about my recovery. Why do some people with an incomplete spinal cord injury get very little return of function, and why do some have significant return, even an approach to normal? The mystery is about what actions best promote healing, compared with what healing happens no matter what you do. It is not my job to solve the mystery, but to live my life as if I have one, not defined by obsession or guilt over disciplines of rehabilitation.

I want to feel my balance without fear and I want the weird, nervy stiffness and spasms in my body to stop. I, like many people in the world, am suffering because of injury, disease, oppression, danger, or loss. Misery is never in short supply in the human condition. I'm hardly near the front of any line of true human misery. This accident was like the weather. Now my story is about who I am with this injury and what happens next and next and next. Can I stand my own company? A life was interrupted one evening in a Mexican beach town, like the glass that is shattered by the wind as it rests on a windowsill. How far is it from this interruption to a life that is more than just possessing a pulse and dressing in the costume of a person?

A TALL MAN with white hair brushed straight back stands with a walker next to a chair pulled out from a table in a café. He unhooks a cushion from his walker and places it on the chair seat. He locks the brake handle on his walker and maneuvers in front of the chair, fingers on the table for balance, then sits and scooches the chair in closer. A shorter man of medium build with graying, wavy hair and a face on the verge of delight enters and casts an appraising eye over his tall friend beside the blue walker. The shorter man comes around, kisses him on the top of his head, pats him on the back, and sits. Before either can speak, a waiter greets them. Without looking at the menu they order. The waiter fills their coffee cups and leaves. The tall man grins. Their conversation isn't the kind you'd overhear in a café. It is the kind that tells a story.

"You've known Jennifer and me from forever. That includes our near wreck on the highway of love. We celebrated our thirtieth wedding anniversary last night."

"(Crossing himself) Holy Mother, Sacre Bleu, Mazel Tov! Defying odds and gravity all at once. Felicidades! But, isn't this like your primero anniversary as the nuevo hombre she's now married to?"

"You mean I should ask her to marry me again, restart the clock?"

"Más o menos. Is there enough left of that guy in the silver picture frame standing at the altar to keep amor vivo? Isn't there a rule of percentages? What are you, fifty percent the same man she vowed to keep? You may have to ask again."

"I hear you. You trying to curdle my eggs and chill my coffee? Does anyone stay fifty percent the same after thirty years? Don't bother answering, theater is full of examples of those who don't. Do you think all we do is get worse, more pendejo than amigo? But I think you're slapping my strut to prove my lovableness. I own a photograph that relates to your let's-see-if-he's-worth-keeping question."

"They say a man who represents himself in court has a fool for a lawyer. But la esperanza perdura, so describe this photo you wish to submit as evidence."

"The photo shows a young man sitting beside a wooden table on the deck-like roof of a house in the Greek mountain town of Delphi. One foot rests sideways on a knee and his head tilts down. He is reading the *International Herald Tribune* spread open in front of him."

"Por que Delphi?"

"My department in Berkeley created a study center for classical drama, with a six-month course divided between Athens and Delphi. I spent the first three months in Athens for lectures and reading. Next we went to Delphi to rehearse and perform classical scenes in the ancient theater site and work with members of the Greek National Theatre. In the photo my hair is cut short and I have a beard. I'm trying to look like the German bad boy, Bertolt Brecht. (*The waiter returns with their food.*) No, he has the over easy. Mine's the huevos. (*The waiter refills their coffee cups.*) Thanks, we're good."

"Que no, bad boy? The one she liked perdido? Ya sabes that wooden soldier is asleep in the infirmary? Qué tan mal can you be?"

"Aren't you sweet to remind me. Even then, all pose. No real bad boy answered the roll call with my name. Forget that. It's about time and place. The year was 1967. I call the Greek Junta as my witness. They seized power, helped by our CIA when the US freaked out that the Communists could win the national election."

"Cierto?"

"It was to the Greek teachers in my program. Not sure about *fact* fact."

"You taste realpolitik with your Horiatiki. That's what you get when you viajar al este for foreign foods. Better to stay in the library and read about it."

"Realpolitik was in Athens where they set up machine guns and sandbags in traffic circles. Delphi is a sleepy little town for tourists, high up on a mountainside. Its fame comes from having one of the most powerful ancient sites, the Oracle of Delphi, your chosen talking psycho profession in an ancient version, the Pythia, the priestess, a she, answering questions with prophecy. See Sophocles's *Oedipus*."

"I object, your honor, relevance."

"I'm getting to it. I woke in the morning to the sound of a braying donkey standing under an olive tree next to my rented room. Yes, we ate horiatiki salads for lunch outdoors on a hillside at weathered wooden tables with the ancient tragedians' sweat in the olive oil. We built masks and costumes for our study scenes. At rehearsal when we watched masked actors come alive in a space and with words conceived more than two thousand years before, it made the hair on our arms stand up."

"Loco Americano goes native. And you, intelligente romántico, still won't cállate about the Greeks."

"Watching the junta round up Greeks and haul them off in ships to an island prison put a chill on the romance."

"Your honor, my worthy colleague has perdió su camino."

"I'm not lost, be patient. I am a Greek geek, and you have me on the romantic. I directed a scene from Sophocles's *Electra*. By treading the same ground as the vase painters, the land of the unbridled Dionysus, I understood that the disasters and suffering imagined in the tragedies had nothing to do with the passion of Christ or the pieties of our civic morality."

"Eso es un gran pensamiento for a grisly domestic tragedy. Sister Electra eggs on Orestes, reluctant brother, to kill mommy. He does the deed and goes mad. Front-page tabloid material."

"Exactamente, except today we use the lurid details to gin up outrage or disgust, without a fearless poetry able to see it without judgment and with pity and fear, to swipe a phrase from Aristotle. It comes from a concept of tragedy encompassing madness and implacable catastrophe, with no lifting of skirts to leap on a chair in fright, or to spew righteous blame. To see it in its ancient home is a chance to feel in my body the shape and weight of a world alive to a belief that ferocious change can visit any man or woman, that it destroys their hold on life to reveal a humanity that contains the strength to remain standing in the aftermath."

"Muy grandioso. Too much ouzo and thin mountain air. I'll sum up for the court. Those who claim dominion on two legs will also comer mierda in the name of change? This is why you don't need to propose again? Your honor, my learned colleague has ancient Greek fairy dust on his brain?"

"Maybe a certain person dying for our sins doesn't explain it all. Anyway, what's the point of school if you don't rub up against something muy grandioso? It was the sixties. The American egg cracked open. Nixon and Kissinger fit the world of Euripides."

"Objection, your honor. Stating an opinion."

"Berkeley plays the part of Athens, oppressed by a facile tyrant, glamor boy Ronnie from the movies?"

"Who are you in this telenovela?"

"I was scum, the American kind, leaking from the cracked egg. My contemporaries were being drafted to fight in a jungle war against people who were as foreign to them as Martians. I held a 2S student deferment and a high draft number. I suspect the reach of my father on my small-town draft board. My cast's righteous fury when Nixon invaded Cambodia nearly destroyed my thesis project."

"Por que es the sixties whirlwind pertinente para ti?"

"It gave juice to being open to change and risk. It made me choose my ground to stand on. It made me want New Mexico, to translate the Greeks to the high desert, this place of ancient rites and atom splitting, to risk colliding with a transformative spirit called Jennifer thus making last night's anniversary possible. I'm still swoonable. Don't bother, I admit it's opinion. I rest my case?"

"Tienes mucho suerte she's the judge. You make fifty percent seem more. Adios. Mazel tov on thirty years. Gracias for the archaeological dig into your photo. We want, so hacemos una historia."

"Sé bueno. It'll be my turn to pay next. Amor a tu esposa."

He stands, pushes off the table with his right hand, and takes hold of his walker. He stands still, straightening against tight, screeching muscles. He hangs the seat cushion on the handle and exits. Outside he walks to his van, takes out his keys, and punches the unlock button that opens the side sliding door. He opens the driver's door and slips the keys and his phone into the hollow of the inside door grip. He tilts up the walker's front wheels and slides the walker in and secures it.

He puts one foot on the running board, brings up his other foot, twists his bottom toward the seat and plunks down, then swings his legs inside. He pushes a button that closes the side door. He reaches around for the seatbelt against scratchy pain in his left shoulder. He retrieves the car keys from the door and starts the engine. He turns off an alarm that says a wheelchair is not locked down in the space the passenger seat has reoccupied. He pushes play on an iPod. An audiobook starts up where it left off. He backs up and drives off.

IF A GREEN SHOOT grows into a bush, or a chick into a chicken, or a toddler into a teenager, we think that represents time passing. You give someone your phone number and he or she is all you think about. If you keep looking at your phone, are you experiencing time passing, time stuck, or desire? You are old and ready to be taken care of. You ask your three daughters to tell you how much they love you so you can allocate your wealth according to their declarations; however, the youngest daughter won't play the game because that is not how love stays true. What follows is ruin. Is time seen in that consequence? When we are older we want a story of our lives: not when we did this or when that happened, but the good stuff—nasty triumphs and glorious fuck-ups; best-laid plans wrecked in a thrill ride; steamy love, with bodies mashing in the dark; lies and secrets; the road marked danger and the lover's leap; ghosts rattling doors; wits saving the day; ambition bared. Tell us the story of what passions can be traced to us, who are they that made us. Time's currents tear at the boat bearing our story. Story is a compass, a way to steer across the secrets and desires, the losses and cruelty, to stay a course and find a harboring shore. Without story, we can't overcome loss to close a chapter and begin again. Story can costume time's random flood, transforming it into shapes we name and to which we give meaning. I'm telling a story. Am I hiding something? I'm not a tabloid. To hide something and show it at the same time is the reason you make a costume.

I reach into my past and rummage for a way to see behind my own practiced mask. I feel for seams and cracks to pry off what I fashioned to cover my fears, ignorance, bad behavior, and mess of conflicted doings. What else? I look with a clear eye on how I am as a physical body: an obduracy of blood and sinew, of muscle and skin and brain and nerves. I consider how I fear this body, and how I am thrilled and feel betrayed by it. I own an arithmetic of being that hates subtraction and makes addition out of the tiniest achievement, each accomplishment a sign of overcoming scratched in the dirt, a mark to keep away the dark and the bear it hides. I want to tell my story so I can glimpse at what makes my life without diminishing its wantingness, its size, its blind energy, its still and electric pleasure, its earnest, fragile goodness, its cruel calculations, its thoughtless stupidities. I want a story that calls out my habits of dodgy talk and judgments pulled straight out of my ass, that admits to taking pleasure in the feelings of hate, in not doing my homework and in the doing of it. I must convey my churning need for other people and the danger of this feeling's opposite, and the need to practice the knowledge that words and touch are different, one is not a substitute for the other.

Nothing I do can prevent suffering as my necessary companion. I leave room for the fool and the skeptic to live under my coifed roof. With luck, contentment will play the role of physician, ministering with the intent to do no harm. But harm can't be avoided. I've come to

know that pulling away the covers and seeing what's beneath isn't easy or without consequence. As the teller of
my story, I can't help hiding something of myself. This
happens not by deceit, but because I live in the middle
of a forest of my own making. Is that a kind of deceit?
It is in your hands if you are inclined to disentangle the
undergrowth, see what I cannot, and know of me something I do not.

Now the story has to end; otherwise, it's just going to
be more. I have another bit to say before we all get up
and go our way. I warned you the picture is pretty and
sometimes not. There are many things I can't explain
or don't understand about my lot. If you think I make
a brave face as we part, well, the truth is . . . what? Both
fair and sometimes not.

There is no note, no signature, that will stop the day
from dawning, and where would we go with our excuse?
There is no other place, no escape, and why would we
want one? Look outside at every creature seizing its place,
taking its breath, unconscious of any doubt. When night
comes, we sleep; then we open our eyes for the morning.
That will do for change, one day to the next—a small
arithmetic. As children, we yearn for the next thing, the
future that glows: when I am bigger I can do this and do
that; surely that will make me happy. But change comes
on us bright and cutting as a diamond.

We are not creatures that crawl in the leaves and
the dirt, nor beasts that rut and bellow. We are things
of mind and sinew that must connect. We connect to
touch, to speech, and to our passion. Other people are
our world. Nothing can save us from that, nor should we
want it to. We endure the weather, the passage of time,
and happenstance, but the heart is shaped by change
made with and by other people. You will not find laugh-

ter, or play, or cruelty, or song, or dizzy love in nature's landscape, at least not the kind you will practice. What we make is drawn by love or the lack of it, and our desire to live in peace within it.

We gain little by worrying or comparing whether it is easy or hard to make our way in this terrain. To be free is to accept that the gifts of happiness will be unequal, will form the struggle that makes us what we are. When I was in the midst of the game—teaching, living my life with Jennifer, the children chasing their own dreams, caught up in ambition—I wrote this poem.

Hey, Hey

No layin' beside the juice pitcher the sun
all dreamy and forgetful. No, the eyes are wide,
the days are short, the iron is hot. Way over the hill
is rest and the valley, is peace in the mind. The dog howls,
the dust is thick, the days a blur, so and so on.
Yes the moon comes up and the sun goes down,
Hey, Hey, we'll all gather round.

You met this guy, off and away, just down the road
Beside the never before and the always again.
He kissed you, and he kissed you, and he kissed you,
He then did leave, and then did not, lips did smack.
Hiking along the no matter no how,
little ones whirl and spin free. Somehow

in the foggy foggy dew you knew, lit a fuse.
So now, it's all dreamy, all schmushed and cheeky,
All fevered and creamy in the creases,
all wonderful and hard.
Hey, Hey, here is there in the yell and shout.
'Til the moon is down and the sun is up.

No more tests, no million in the mail,
no I shoulda coulda, No, No, just us
the you and me and babies make glee,
The call of the wild, the whackado, and the old ones.
Hey, Hey, We're a pair, Yes, Yes.

Scratch a match, pierce the dark. squeeze the dirt,
Sing for all souls here below, pray no child's in the dark.
After the moon comes up and the sun is down
Yes, Yes all turned over, wondered and round.

When I was a boy I learned to ride a bike, but my mother's rules confined me to the territory of our driveway. She didn't feel safe letting me loose on the rural roads around our house. One summer day, after my mother fed my friends lunch, I put her on the spot in front of them with a desperate plea: "Let me go with these guys, please, please, their mothers let them." I ended on a maximum whiny pitch and sad look. She lifted the ban and I left with my friends in a jostle of excitement. Home was on a hill, separated from a lake below by an old path that ran through our property down to a dirt road bordering a lake. That's where we headed. We pedaled happily along the road. I was in the rear. Your Honor, this is Exhibit A, if it please the court. It will show that a man bearing my name showed he was a naïve congregant by closing his eyes to thank the unnamed powers ruling the world for release from his front yard. In the midst of this eyes closed mumbling, he veered off the road and crashed into a ditch. No damage done, he picked himself up, embarrassed, and yelled about bees. He pleads guilty, Your Honor, to driving under the influence of a naïve heart and excess virtue.

I am not straining toward organ chords but toward

lightness. To be human is to know and carry loss throughout our lives. The one who stood up after falling off an
ordinary porch has no choice but to be different. What I
can do is pick up as many pieces as will fit into my hand,
miss the ones that won't fit, and make new ones. The new
will accept the damage and trouble my body causes every
day. The new can't become stones to polish for sympathy or an exception, excusing me from the hurly-burly
that life offers. Thinking is no excuse for not washing
the dishes or practicing a civil tongue. Doing so will not
mean I'm not afraid, that I don't have bouts of fury or
doubt my strength to make the effort to stay engaged.
I can't make up for the impact this has on Jennifer. She
hasn't asked me to.

I know now that after a fall it is not so easy to jump
up, brush yourself off, and join in again. I know life is
cruel and capricious, with equal measures of goodness.
Where I fell as an adult is lush with palm trees, has
wide, sandy beaches and achingly blue water that teems
with giant whales elegantly traveling to their breeding
grounds. That one bad thing happens does not change
the fact that one good thing happens, that these circumstances occur next to each other by seconds. There is no
logic or belief that makes sense of this. There is only per-
sistence, patience, and the wonder of our connection to
others who miraculously love us as we love them. Is this
enough to keep us in the game, a game we know has no
certain rules?

A wind blew over the cocktail glass I placed on my
windowsill as I prepared for Mexico with Jennifer. It
shattered on the floor. That wind is still there, outside
my window. But I have other glasses. I can still make a
cocktail. The ingredients will be different. The window-

sill is still there as I set down a new glass. In the faded light I can see the trees that border the river. There are tracks along the edge in soft ground where the bear walks at night.

Acknowledgments

FRIENDS WHO RESPONDED to my weekly writings after I was injured encouraged this book, in particular my friend Sam Roll and my son Matt. Matt wrote me a letter when he thought I was in a spiritual retreat to encourage me to write. He said, "There is meaning in your suffering. It's up to you to define it. I care. I want to know what you have to say. I have no preconceptions about what it might mean. I only hope that you surprise me and that it allows me into your experience as fully as possible." For this book to succeed with the reader, it will need to meet this hope. Sam, who read an early section of the book when I felt vulnerable about the project, told me, "This is your own good story told in your own good way," a deft palm on the forehead to calm the skittish horse in the gate. I want to thank my friends Bev Magennis and Elsa Menendez, who read the book in draft form and gave me valuable notes. I am again indebted to my insightful friend Jim Danneskiold, who if I'm writing has my back with his editorial expertise. The book found its champion in the accomplished editor, Beth Hadas. Thanks to her savvy, the book found its form and saw a way this most personal project could be published when fortune was ready to faint from the effort. Grateful thanks to Julia Sippel of Paul Dry Books, whose editorial craft took the fabric of this book and connected stray misaligned threads and sharpened the cut of the cloth. Without Paul Dry of the press by his name there would be no light of day for this story, my thanks.

I want to acknowledge two women who put me on the path of recovery at a time when no such thing looked possible. They worked with me through my entire time at Craig Hospital as my physical therapist and my occupational therapist. Meghan Joyce and Caitlin Glennon are two remarkable young women who found me a wreck and never let what they found have the power to define me. When I came home from the hospital, Lisa Glasknap was my morning companion as home health-care helper. Her sure-handed care bridged an anxious time. By arrangement of a small, busy household god, my first driver was a young man from Maine, Marc McCourt. We connected as two Pine Tree State familiars, and he eased my return to the outside world. Caroline Hess was my second driver and assistant for most of a year, taking me hither and yon, including back to Craig for my upgrade. She is herself no stranger to the effects of illness. She is a lively, resourceful friend who always seemed to have a tool belt for whatever problem arose. I made a new friend, Colleen Cummins, because of my injury. She works to give my body back to me using her expertise as a Pilates therapist. She is like a weaver from fairy tales who can knit together the threads of brain and body into mind. There are two lives exposed here: that of Jennifer, my wife and partner, and mine. There is no life as I know it without her.